Hand Reading in Bridge

How To Improve Your Card Play

Danny Roth's new book covers, in the author's familiar style, many important areas of declarer's play and defence. The main theme is 'vision' at the bridge table. With the aid of 55 stimulating problem hands, the author tackles the delicate task of looking through the backs of the cards to determine the enemy holdings. It is only when you have learned to 'see' the opponents' cards and read their intentions that you have a good chance of devising countermeasures.

A study of this book may not make you a dab hand at palmistry, but there is no doubt that your card play will benefit considerably.

Hand Reading in Bridge
How To Improve Your Card Play

Danny Roth

LONDON
VICTOR GOLLANCZ
in association with
PETER CRAWLEY

First published in Great Britain 1993
in association with Peter Crawley
by Victor Gollancz
An imprint of Cassell
Villiers House, 41–47 Strand, London WC2N 5JE

A catalogue record for this book
is available from the British Library

ISBN 0 575 05434 4

Photoset in Great Britain by
Rowland Phototypesetting Ltd, Bury St Edmunds, Suffolk
and printed by St Edmundsbury Press Ltd,
Bury St Edmunds, Suffolk

Hand Reading in Bridge

How To Improve Your Card Play

A good pair of X-ray eyes.

Isn't that what every bridge player so badly needs? Sadly, not even with the untold wonders of modern technology is this an item which one can walk into a shop and order. Worse still, even if it were, the bridge authorities would lose little time in banning it. Legal X-ray eyes have to be developed over a long period as a bridge player learns his skill, and the intention of my books has been to help readers in this quest.

'Practice makes perfect!' as the old saying goes and the purpose of reading books is to play and defend hands by yourself, free of rebuke from partners and team-mates, in as near match conditions as possible and then to look at the full deal when we can conduct the post-mortem with the impeccable politeness you would like to see at the table.

I therefore offer you another set of problems presented in quiz form—you are shown your hand and dummy's, South always being declarer. Imagine that you are playing a multiple teams event or series of team-of-four matches. You will meet a variety of bidding systems and styles over a season and all bidding will be carefully explained. You should assume that you are playing in top-class company, but remember the other three players are, like yourself, human beings and capable of making mistakes.

As is customary, we shall start with a gentle warm-up hand to give you an illustration of the format. Take the West seat—you will be dealing at love all.

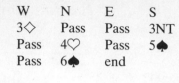

W	N	E	S
3◇	Pass	Pass	3NT
Pass	4♡	Pass	5♠
Pass	6♠	end	

♠ Q J 10 9 4
♡ K 6 3
◇ 6 3
♣ K Q 9

♠ 3
♡ Q J 7
◇ K J 10 9 8 7 4
♣ 5 2

After South's natural three no-trump bid, North transferred to spades but South was obviously good for his first bid so he invited a slam.

You lead the ♣5 to the nine, ten and ace. South returns the ♡2 to dummy's king, partner dropping the ten, and plays the queen of trumps to the two, five and three. On the jack of trumps, partner produces the eight and South the six. What do you discard?

I have discussed defensive signalling at some length in previous books but briefly, signals fall into four main categories:
a) encouragement or discouragement of the suit led;
b) distribution (usually odd or even) of the suit led;
c) suit preference;
d) other important information like honour holdings and side-suit lengths.

On this occasion, with your having opened three diamonds, South's having bid three no-trumps and your having failed to lead diamonds, it should be clear to partner that you have a tenace over South as here:

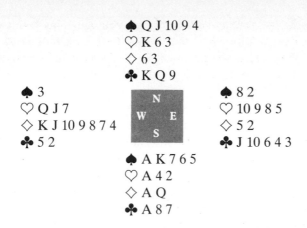

♠ Q J 10 9 4
♡ K 6 3
◇ 6 3
♣ K Q 9

♠ 3
♡ Q J 7
◇ K J 10 9 8 7 4
♣ 5 2

N
W   E
S

♠ 8 2
♡ 10 9 8 5
◇ 5 2
♣ J 10 6 4 3

♠ A K 7 6 5
♡ A 4 2
◇ A Q
♣ A 8 7

A good way to confirm the position is to discard the ◇J. This
clearly denies the queen and promises the ten—coming under
the heading d) above. Was that your choice?

Let us think a little further. Did you notice anything strange
about the play so far? Declarer won the first trick in hand and
then crossed to dummy in hearts to play those trumps. Why
didn't he win the club on dummy to play trumps immediately? If
you asked yourself that question, you are well on the way to
realising 'what on earth is going on here?' The inverted commas
surround what I call the 'Magic question' and if only players,
both declarers and defenders, asked themselves that question
a little more often, the mistakes avoided would run into
thousands.

What you had to realise was that, while drawing trumps was
very urgent, playing that round of hearts was far more important.
If you look back at the deal, you can see why. Declarer plans to
draw trumps, eliminate clubs, cash the ♡A and throw you in
with the third round to force you to lead away from your

diamonds. In order to avoid the disaster, you must play your two honours on the first two rounds of hearts so that partner can win the third. When I set the problem, I asked you what you would play to trick four. What I really wanted to know was which card you played to trick two!

If you played the seven, the hand is over. You cannot recover by discarding one of your heart honours on the trump because then South cashes the other heart, eliminates clubs, cashes the ◇A and exits with the queen to your king, forcing you to give a ruff and discard—and that is not to mention the alternative double-dummy line of eliminating clubs and exiting with a low heart to force you to open up the diamonds.

It is in the respect of not necessarily asking for your play at the critical moment, that I differ from other authors on play and defence. It is an attempt to get nearer to match conditions when there is nobody to give you the timely nudge. Had I phrased the problem: '. . . declarer wins the opening club lead in hand and plays the ♡2. Which card do you play?', you would have undoubtedly realised that this was your big moment and very probably have produced the right answer. But I should be surprised if you did so the first time—unless, of course, you are one of my hardened readers. Notice, by the way, partner's ♡10, confirming that he had the nine and that it was safe for you to continue the unblock. I try to impress my students that, even with very poor hands like East's, you should play a full part in the proceedings. When solving problems, do not be content to give your line of play but rather a full dossier on the hand, understanding why play has taken a specific course up to now and how you expect it to continue and far more important—why. No credit for good guessing. All the best!

Hand No. 1

Dealer South
E–W vulnerable

W	N	E	S
			2♣
Pass	2♢	Pass	2NT
Pass	3♣	Pass	3♡
Pass	4♡	end	

♠ J 8 6 2
♡ A 7 5 2
♢ 7 2
♣ 8 7 5

♠ Q 7 4 3
♡ K Q 9 3
♢ A K
♣ A K Q

Your Acol sequence showed 23–24 points balanced and a Baron Roll followed.

West leads the ♣5 and East wins with the king. He follows with the ♠A, on which West discards the ♢6. East then plays the ♠10, ruffed by West with the ♡4. West now switches to the ♣J; plan the play.

After a poor start, it should all be plain sailing now but this is exactly the kind of situation where the unsuspecting declarer can be caught off his guard. The only danger now lies in a possible trump loser which implies that the remaining four trumps must be all in one hand. If West started with all five trumps, there is nothing you can do but if East has the stack, you have a safety play, cashing the ace on dummy first and then taking the two finesses marked against him when West shows out.

The full deal:

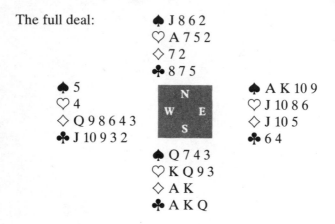

♠ J 8 6 2
♡ A 7 5 2
◇ 7 2
♣ 8 7 5

♠ 5
♡ 4
◇ Q 9 8 6 4 3
♣ J 10 9 3 2

♠ A K 10 9
♡ J 10 8 6
◇ J 10 5
♣ 6 4

♠ Q 7 4 3
♡ K Q 9 3
◇ A K
♣ A K Q

In order to take the second finesse, you will have to return to dummy and that can only be done with the ♠J. You did, of course, anticipate this and carefully played the ♠Q on trick three! If you didn't, one off.

Hand No. 2

Dealer South
N–S vulnerable

W	N	E	S
			2♡
Pass	4♡	end	

♠ K J 7 5
♡ 9 5 2
♢ Q J 3
♣ 8 5 4

♠ A 2
♡ K Q J 10 8 6
♢ 10 2
♣ A K 7

After your Acol two-opener, the direct raise customarily denied
an ace.

West leads ♠10; plan the play.

Counting your tricks, you see five in hearts, two in spades and two in clubs on top to give nine in all and it seems tempting to go for an immediate tenth by taking the free spade finesse now. However, there is a strong case against it. Firstly, even if it works there is no guarantee that you will be able to reach the king on dummy as East might have the ace to three or four trumps. Secondly, and more important, if you play the ♠J now and the queen appears from East, dummy's ♠K can be attacked from either side of the table. Thirdly, it is unlikely that East would lead away from a queen round to an Acol two-opener and therefore an attempt to drop her or ruff her out is hardly a poorer chance.

For these reasons, it is probably better to go for your tenth trick in diamonds and as this will involve losing the lead twice, they must be attacked at once before the defenders establish their club trick. You should therefore win the first spade in hand and lead the ♢10 to enjoy the protected spade tenace in dummy when East has to win the first round.

The full deal:

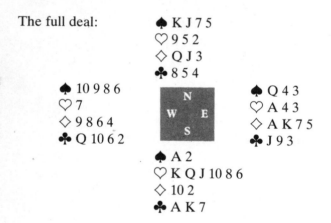

```
                    ♠ K J 7 5
                    ♡ 9 5 2
                    ♢ Q J 3
                    ♣ 8 5 4
  ♠ 10 9 8 6                      ♠ Q 4 3
  ♡ 7             N               ♡ A 4 3
  ♢ 9 8 6 4    W     E            ♢ A K 7 5
  ♣ Q 10 6 2       S             ♣ J 9 3
                    ♠ A 2
                    ♡ K Q J 10 8 6
                    ♢ 10 2
                    ♣ A K 7
```

Should West win the first diamond and continue spades, you should rise with the king and hope the ♡9 will provide an entry to the third diamond.

Hand No. 3

Dealer West
Both vulnerable

W	N	E	S
2♡	Dble	Pass	3♡
Pass	3♠	Pass	5♣
end			

♠ Q 10 8 5 4
♡ K
♢ A K J 5
♣ 10 6 3

♠ J 9
♡ A 4 3
♢ 4 3
♣ A Q J 9 8 5

West's opening bid showed 7–11 points and exactly six hearts to at least one of the top three honours. After partner's take-out double, your cue-bid invited three no-trumps, but sadly your partner did not consider a singleton king good enough. So a rare event has occurred—you are in the wrong contract.

West leads the ♡Q; plan the play.

There are two possible lines. One is to take the trump finesse, hoping to concede just two spade tricks; the other is to take the diamond finesse, hoping to discard a spade on the third round. The usual rule in situations where two finesses are available and there isn't time to take both, is to play for the drop in the suit where you are longest (i.e., where you have a better chance of success) so that you can hold the lead and then take the finesse in the other. On winning the heart in dummy, you should play a club to the ace and if the king fails to appear, try the diamond finesse.

The full deal:

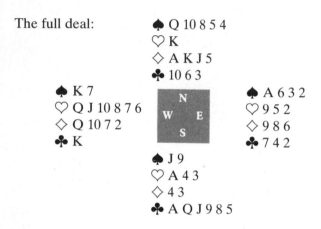

♠ Q 10 8 5 4
♡ K
♢ A K J 5
♣ 10 6 3

♠ K 7
♡ Q J 10 8 7 6
♢ Q 10 7 2
♣ K

♠ A 6 3 2
♡ 9 5 2
♢ 9 8 6
♣ 7 4 2

♠ J 9
♡ A 4 3
♢ 4 3
♣ A Q J 9 8 5

This line is likely to be best although it is true that, as East is known to hold three cards in hearts against West's six, a finesse against East in clubs is more likely to succeed. Against that, however, it is clear that, on the opening lead, West is most unlikely to hold both spade honours and he may well need at least one of the minor-suit honours to make up the points needed for his bid, i.e., unless he has exactly the ♠A to go with the ♡ Q J for a bare minimum.

Note that, if West has only Q x in diamonds, all is not necessarily lost; he might have started with ♣ K x, after which he will have to ruff the third round with the ♣K. An opening lead of the ♠K would, of course, have defeated the contract by a trump promotion on the third round.

Hand No. 4

Dealer South
Both vulnerable

	W	N	E	S
				1♠
	Pass	2◇	Pass	3◇
	Pass	4♠	end	

♠ K 7 3
♡ J 10 6
◇ A Q 9 6 4
♣ 6 2

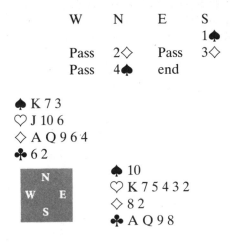

♠ 10
♡ K 7 5 4 3 2
◇ 8 2
♣ A Q 9 8

Partner leads the ♣J to dummy's two; plan your defence.

You are distressed to note that a great deal seems to be well-placed for declarer. When roll-calling in this situation, it is best to assume that potentially badly-placed cards are with declarer. The ♢K is a case in point. If partner has it, South will need the ♡A to justify his bidding so those two cards should be placed the other way round. The only factor that could hurt declarer is the bad trump split and a forcing game is called for. Thus hearts must be attacked and the best card, after winning the club trick, is the king. That will leave partner's ace behind the shortage if South has the queen and declarer can be forced twice, losing control.

The full deal:

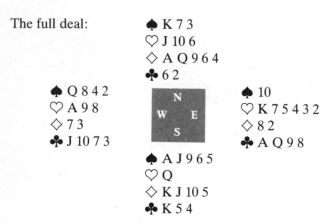

```
                        ♠ K 7 3
                        ♡ J 10 6
                        ♢ A Q 9 6 4
                        ♣ 6 2
    ♠ Q 8 4 2                              ♠ 10
    ♡ A 9 8           N                    ♡ K 7 5 4 3 2
    ♢ 7 3          W     E                 ♢ 8 2
    ♣ J 10 7 3        S                    ♣ A Q 9 8
                        ♠ A J 9 6 5
                        ♡ Q
                        ♢ K J 10 5
                        ♣ K 5 4
```

Note that, if you play a low heart, declarer prevails. With the king, however, only the double-dummy line of running the ♠J will give him a chance. When this hand turned up in a county match, East (who had driven a very long way to 'enjoy' the match) was very proud to find this defence, but West could only turn up with ♠ J x x x! Now declarer ruffed the second heart, played the king and another club for a ruff and followed with three rounds of trumps before playing on diamonds to cruelly turn the forcing game on us. Virtue is its own reward, they say!

Hand No. 5

Dealer East
N–S vulnerable

W	N	E	S
		Pass	1♡
Pass	2♣	Pass	2♠
Pass	3♠	Pass	4◇
Pass	5♣	Pass	6♠
end			

♠ A Q 8 2
♡ 5
◇ 8 6 4
♣ A K 8 6 3

♠ K 9 7 4
♡ A Q 8 7 6
◇ A K Q
♣ Q

Following your game-forcing reverse, cue-bidding led to the slam.

West leads the ◇J to the four, three and ace. All follow to the ♠K; how do you continue?

The first point to realise is that, if the trumps break, you cannot be denied five trumps tricks, three clubs, a heart and three diamonds to total twelve so you must assume that someone will show out on the next round. In that case, you should try to combine the chances of setting up a long club or the heart finesse. Cash the ♣Q now and cross to the ♠A. Ruff a club in hand and cash the other two top diamonds before playing a third round of trumps. Now start cashing the clubs from the top. If they break, there is no problem; if not, whoever ruffs will either have to lead a heart, allowing you a (possibly free) finesse, or the last diamond, which enables you to ruff in dummy and take the heart finesse yourself.

The full deal:

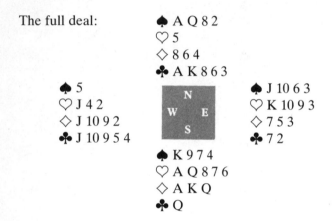

```
                    ♠ A Q 8 2
                    ♡ 5
                    ◇ 8 6 4
                    ♣ A K 8 6 3
   ♠ 5                           ♠ J 10 6 3
   ♡ J 4 2            N          ♡ K 10 9 3
   ◇ J 10 9 2      W   E         ◇ 7 5 3
   ♣ J 10 9 5 4       S          ♣ 7 2
                    ♠ K 9 7 4
                    ♡ A Q 8 7 6
                    ◇ A K Q
                    ♣ Q
```

Hand No. 6

Dealer South
Neither vulnerable

W	N	E	S
			1♡
Pass	Pass	1♠	3♣
3♠	5♣	end	

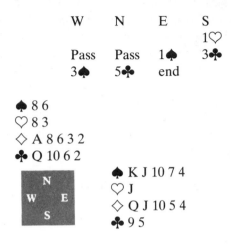

♠ 8 6
♡ 8 3
◇ A 8 6 3 2
♣ Q 10 6 2

♠ K J 10 7 4
♡ J
◇ Q J 10 5 4
♣ 9 5

North–South are playing Precision style so South's bidding is likely to show at least 5–5 in his two suits and about 14–15 points.

It is rare that, once a limited one-level bid has been passed, your innocent protective overcall should propel the opponents into game at the five level. However, that is what has happened and partner leads the ♠A and continues with the queen when you encourage, South following with the two and three; plan your defence.

The bidding and early play give you an accurate roll-call on the hand. Partner's second spade indicates an initial holding of a trebleton, leaving South also with three and therefore a diamond void. You see that South cannot start ruffing hearts in dummy until he has drawn your trumps, after which he will have only two trumps left in dummy to ruff three losers. You should thus realise that South has no hope unless his intermediate hearts are better than partner's and he can take what will become marked ruffing finesses after you have shown out on the second round. To prevent this, you should take charge of the defence by overtaking in spades and playing a third round. A spade ruff in dummy is the last thing declarer wants (he could discard his loser on the ◇A). Reduced to one trump on dummy available for ruffing hearts, he will have to concede a trick to partner.

The full deal:

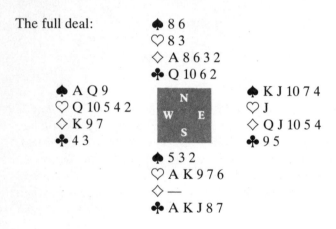

```
                    ♠ 8 6
                    ♡ 8 3
                    ◇ A 8 6 3 2
                    ♣ Q 10 6 2
    ♠ A Q 9                        ♠ K J 10 7 4
    ♡ Q 10 5 4 2       N           ♡ J
    ◇ K 9 7        W       E       ◇ Q J 10 5 4
    ♣ 4 3              S           ♣ 9 5
                    ♠ 5 3 2
                    ♡ A K 9 7 6
                    ◇ —
                    ♣ A K J 8 7
```

Hand No. 7

Dealer East
Neither vulnerable

W	N	E	S
		Pass	1♠
Pass	2♡	Pass	2♠
Pass	3♢	Pass	3NT
	end		

♠ —
♡ A K 7 6 2
♢ A 10 9 6 5 3
♣ 3 2

♠ K Q 7 6 4 2
♡ 9 3
♢ K 7
♣ K Q 5

We could discuss at some length how North should bid his hand, but you seem to have reached a reasonable contract; game in one of the red suits would hardly be an improvement.

West leads the ♣10 to his partner's ace and East returns the jack which you win. How do you continue?

You have two tricks each in clubs and hearts and therefore five will be required in diamonds. In the context of that suit in isolation, the correct play is to start with the king and then run the next round, failing only if East turns up with four or more including both missing honours or West has all five. However, as is so often the case, the 'correct' play in a single suit is not always the best when the whole hand is considered. The danger lies in a possible 4–2 heart break. The defence will win the second or third round of diamonds and exit in hearts, locking you in dummy and depriving you of your second club trick. Eventually you may lose two tricks in hearts and one in each of the other suits. To combat this, you must keep entries in both hands by ducking the first round of diamonds completely. Now, if they play hearts, you can win in dummy, return in diamonds to cash your second club winner in hand and then go back to dummy in hearts to enjoy the rest of the diamonds.

The full deal:

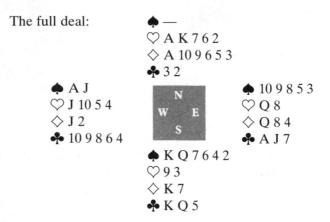

```
                    ♠ —
                    ♡ A K 7 6 2
                    ◇ A 10 9 6 5 3
                    ♣ 3 2
    ♠ A J                          ♠ 10 9 8 5 3
    ♡ J 10 5 4          N          ♡ Q 8
    ◇ J 2          W        E       ◇ Q 8 4
    ♣ 10 9 8 6 4        S          ♣ A J 7
                    ♠ K Q 7 6 4 2
                    ♡ 9 3
                    ◇ K 7
                    ♣ K Q 5
```

Hand No. 8

Dealer East
Both vulnerable

W	N	E	S
		Pass	1♠
Dble	2♦	Pass	4♠
end			

♠ Q 10
♡ 6 2
♦ A K J 10 6 5
♣ 7 4 2

♠ A K J 9 7 6 4
♡ Q 5
♦ Q
♣ A Q 5

In modern style, partner's bid was forcing, as though West had not bid.

West cashes the two top hearts, East following with the three and ten. Now comes the ♦9; plan the play.

The diamond switch has prevented you from taking the rest of the tricks off the top and the danger now is that you will be cut off from the diamonds and be held to seven trump tricks and the two minor aces. One obvious line is to draw trumps, hoping for a 2–2 split. Better is to play one round of trumps, won in dummy and then start on diamonds so that if East ruffs, you can return to dummy with the other trump, drawing his remaining trump in the process and enjoy the rest of the diamonds. That covers a 3–1 trump split. But better still is to win in dummy now and carry on with diamonds immediately. Now you will be successful even against a 4–0 trump stack, and a 5–1 diamond split.

The full deal:

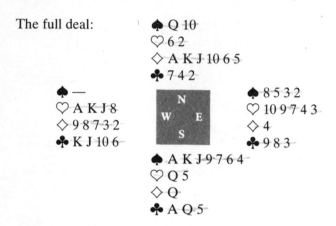

Note East's carding to the two top hearts. The first card gave the count; the second indicated a preference to diamonds, the principal message being inability to help in clubs, which was likely to be the source of further defensive tricks.

Hand No. 9

Dealer West
Both vulnerable

W	N	E	S
Pass	Pass	1♡	2♣
Pass	Pass	Dble	end

♠ J 8 7
♡ 9 6 5
♢ A 10 8 7 5
♣ 8 5

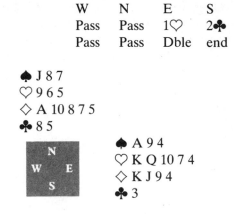

♠ A 9 4
♡ K Q 10 7 4
♢ K J 9 4
♣ 3

Partner leads the ♡8 to the five, queen and ace. South plays the
♠K to the three and seven; plan your defence.

When planning a defence, you should put yourself in South's seat and ask how he proposes to make his contract. In a situation like this, where partner clearly has the trumps heavily stacked, declarer's only hope is to make his trumps by ruffing (in this case diamonds) while partner is obliged to follow suit. Thus you should make every effort to ensure this does not happen, firstly by refusing the ♠A to limit South's entries to dummy and secondly, instead of rushing to give partner an unwanted heart ruff, to start drawing them at once by pushing your lone trump through.

The full deal:

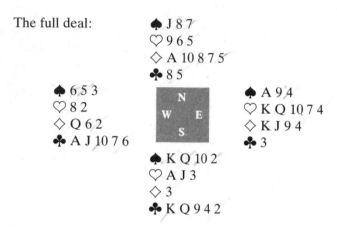

```
              ♠ J 8 7
              ♡ 9 6 5
              ◇ A 10 8 7 5
              ♣ 8 5
♠ 6 5 3                        ♠ A 9 4
♡ 8 2          N               ♡ K Q 10 7 4
◇ Q 6 2    W       E           ◇ K J 9 4
♣ A J 10 7 6       S           ♣ 3
              ♠ K Q 10 2
              ♡ A J 3
              ◇ 3
              ♣ K Q 9 4 2
```

Observe what happens if you make the two mistakes. Whatever West does after the heart ruff, declarer is able to arrange two diamond ruffs in his hand and exits with the last spade at trick ten. Forced to ruff, partner has to give declarer two of the last three trump tricks for the contract. When a similar hand came up in an international match, East's errors were that much more expensive when hearts were trumps! Note that you defeat the contract even if you win the spade too early, provided you push the trump through (West draws a second round and makes four trump tricks in all) or in any event, if you hold the ♠A up to the third round.

Hand No. 10

Dealer South
Neither vulnerable

W	N	E	S
			1♡
Pass	1NT	Dble	Redble
2♣	Dble	2♢	2♠
Pass	3♡	Pass	4♡
Pass			
end			

♠ 10 5 3
♡ K J
♢ 9 6 3 2
♣ K Q 8 4

♠ A K 9 4
♡ 10 9 8 6 4
♢ A
♣ A J 7

West leads the ♢J to the two, seven and ace. You return the ♡4 to the two, jack and East's queen and he persists with the ♢K. You ruff, West following with the five. How do you continue?

The bidding and early play have given you a fairly accurate picture of the distribution. East should have the other major for his take-out double against your heart bid and West's diamond lead was clearly a doubleton, leaving East with six. He must have the ace of trumps for his bid and the only question which arises is whether he is 4–2–6–1 or 4–3–6–0. There are two factors which point to the former. Firstly, it is already dangerous to make a take-out double with a singleton in a side suit, never mind a void but more important, with a club void and ♡ A Q x, East would surely have doubled the final contract and it would have been obvious to West what was required.

You are thus in a position to play double dummy.

The full deal:

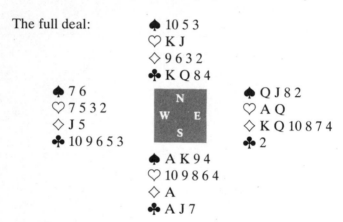

```
                    ♠ 10 5 3
                    ♡ K J
                    ◇ 9 6 3 2
                    ♣ K Q 8 4
  ♠ 7 6                              ♠ Q J 8 2
  ♡ 7 5 3 2          N              ♡ A Q
  ◇ J 5          W       E          ◇ K Q 10 8 7 4
  ♣ 10 9 6 5 3        S              ♣ 2
                    ♠ A K 9 4
                    ♡ 10 9 8 6 4
                    ◇ A
                    ♣ A J 7
```

Ten tricks are there in three trumps, two top spades, the diamond and four clubs but the problem is in timing. If you carry on with trumps now, East will win and force you with a further diamond. You will have to ruff and West will discard a spade and remain with longer trumps than yours. You will still be able to cash your four club tricks, but only one of the spades. Cashing two top spades and then playing trumps is no good either. East will win, cash a third spade and lead a fourth round which West can ruff.

The solution is to cash the two top spades and play on clubs immediately. East can ruff at any time and cash his spade, but he cannot prevent you from ruffing your fourth spade in dummy, holding him to three tricks. If he allows three or four clubs to stand up, you will be able to discard a spade on the fourth round, conceding a heart and a spade at the finish.

Hand No. 11

Dealer North
E–W vulnerable

W	N	E	S
	Pass	Pass	1♡
Pass	3◇	Pass	4♡
end			

♠ —
♡ K 7 2
◇ Q J 8 5 3
♣ A J 9 6 3

South's opening bid may only be a four-card major with 12–16 points (Blue Club style). North's jump indicates good trump support and a diamond suit. Partner is likely to turn up with a large number of spades and at adverse vulnerability, you wisely decide not to overcall or make an unusual no-trump (forcing the bidding to the three-level and thereby asking for trouble), particularly when partner has already passed.

What do you lead?

In this kind of situation, players tend to start racking their brains as to the best chance of getting their partner in to get the spade ruff. With North having promised good diamonds, a case could be made for underleading the ♣A. But it is far better to consider the whole hand. How is declarer going to make this contract? Your heavy diamond stack rules out many tricks in that suit and it is clear that declarer will not get rich on clubs either. Neither opponent showed much interest in spades and in any case, you know that they could not be breaking more unfavourably. It thus seems that declarer's best chance lies in a crossruff and you should forgo your ruffing potential by trying to destroy his and lead a trump.

The full deal:

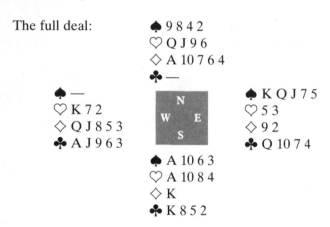

```
                      ♠ 9 8 4 2
                      ♡ Q J 9 6
                      ◇ A 10 7 6 4
                      ♣ —
     ♠ —                              ♠ K Q J 7 5
     ♡ K 7 2           N              ♡ 5 3
     ◇ Q J 8 5 3    W     E           ◇ 9 2
     ♣ A J 9 6 3       S              ♣ Q 10 7 4
                      ♠ A 10 6 3
                      ♡ A 10 8 4
                      ◇ K
                      ♣ K 8 5 2
```

This is likely to lead to two off—when declarer, organising club ruffs, crosses to his hand with the ♠A, you will be able to ruff and lead your last trump to hold him to eight tricks. To rub further salt into the wound regarding the spade ruff, let us replay the hand with North as declarer. East leads the 'obvious' ♠K and you ruff the ace—what now? Yes, it has to be a trump; otherwise declarer takes two diamond tricks and eight more on the crossruff. Who said: 'Never lead away from a doubleton king!'?

Hand No. 12

Dealer West
E–W vulnerable

W	N	E	S
1NT	3◇	Pass	3NT
end			

♠ 9 4
♡ 9 2
◇ K 10 8 7 6 5 3
♣ A K

♠ A Q 6 3
♡ K Q J 5
◇ Q
♣ 7 5 3 2

Your opponents are playing a variable no-trump, so West's opening bid showed 15–17. North's overcall was of intermediate strength, having been debarred from bidding two diamonds as that would have shown a two-suiter, including spades.

West leads the ♣Q to the ace, nine and two; your opponents' style is to show distribution when following to partner's lead. How do you continue and would it make any difference if dummy had produced the ◇J instead of the ◇10? Is anything in the book's introduction relevant to this hand?

You are in a very poor contract and even if the spade finesse is right (and it obviously is not) you will be nowhere near nine tricks unless dummy's diamonds can be brought in. The inevitable club lead has removed a vital entry prematurely and prospects are now even dimmer.

In situations like this, you must take the liberty of assuming that the cards lie exactly as you want them, bearing in mind that your assumption must be consistent with the bidding and play so far. Here the only hope is to find West with exactly $\diamondsuit$ A J doubleton but even now, the suit must be played with care. Leading it from dummy allows West to duck after which you are an entry short. For that reason, you must cross to hand with the $\spadesuit$A, holding the lead to avoid an early second round of clubs, and lead the $\diamondsuit$Q from hand. Now if West ducks, you can overtake and clear the suit.

The full deal:

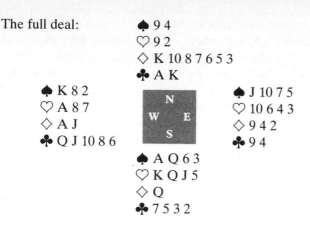

```
                        ♠ 9 4
                        ♡ 9 2
                        ◇ K 10 8 7 6 5 3
                        ♣ A K
♠ K 8 2                                    ♠ J 10 7 5
♡ A 8 7           N                        ♡ 10 6 4 3
◇ A J         W       E                    ◇ 9 4 2
♣ Q J 10 8 6          S                    ♣ 9 4
                        ♠ A Q 6 3
                        ♡ K Q J 5
                        ◇ Q
                        ♣ 7 5 3 2
```

If North has the ◇J instead of the ten, you have a better chance, but you should still play the suit the same way. Starting with the king from dummy will not be good enough as West can now win and play a second club while the defenders still have a second diamond stopper. So let us replay the hand. The lead is won by dummy's ♣K; you cross to the ♠A and lead the ◇Q. West plays the two, dummy the king and East the nine. How do you continue and would it make any difference if West's first card had been the four? You now have to decide whether to play West for ◇ A 2 doubleton (i.e., a low diamond now) or East for ◇ 10 9 doubleton (i.e., the ◇ J now). Much depends on your assessment of the quality of your opponents. In the introduction, I asked you to imagine that you were playing in a top-class field. In that case, East should drop the nine or ten on the first round from (◇ 10 9 x) to give you a losing option.

It is my experience that only top international players would find this defence and even then it is very easy to lose interest in the proceedings when defending with a hand as poor as East's (you, of course, know better by now!). If you are playing against county standard or weaker players, I suggest you should play ◇J on the second round. How about West? Not many people would play the ◇4 from ◇ A 4 2, even in top-class circles. I should recommend trusting the four as a true card and playing low on the second round. If West plays the two, then your play depends on your opinion of East. Initially, it appears that West started with five clubs and East two so if you still cannot decide, the odds favour West having the shortage, i.e., a low card on the second round.

Hand No. 13

Dealer East
N–S vulnerable

W	N	E	S
		2♠	3NT
Pass	4NT	Pass	6♢
end			

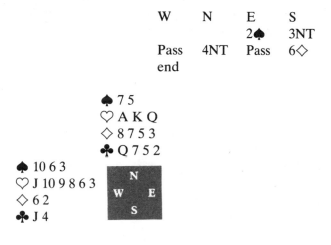

```
              ♠ 7 5
              ♡ A K Q
              ♢ 8 7 5 3
              ♣ Q 7 5 2
♠ 10 6 3        ┌─────┐
♡ J 10 9 8 6 3  │  N  │
♢ 6 2           │ W E │
♣ J 4           │  S  │
                └─────┘
```

Partner's opening bid showed 6–9 points with exactly six spades to at least one of the top three honours. South's 3NT showed at least 20 points and his partner's raise was quantitative.

You lead the ♡J to the ace, five and four. South draws trumps in two rounds, partner following low and then cashes the ace and king of spades and the other two hearts, partner discarding two spades. Now follows the ♣Q from dummy, covered by the king and ace and South exits with the ♣6.

Have you any comment on the play so far and how do you plan your defence?

The bidding and early play have placed East with 6–1–2–4. South clearly has eleven tricks on top and the twelfth hangs on the club suit. If South has the ten, there is no hope for you, but if partner has it and the eight or nine as well, the defence can take two club tricks now, provided you have unblocked your jack under the other honours. If you still have it, you are forced to concede a ruff and discard and the contract,

The full deal:

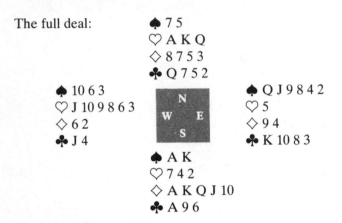

```
                    ♠ 7 5
                    ♡ A K Q
                    ♢ 8 7 5 3
                    ♣ Q 7 5 2
    ♠ 10 6 3              N        ♠ Q J 9 8 4 2
    ♡ J 10 9 8 6 3     W     E     ♡ 5
    ♢ 6 2                 S        ♢ 9 4
    ♣ J 4                          ♣ K 10 8 3
                    ♠ A K
                    ♡ 7 4 2
                    ♢ A K Q J 10
                    ♣ A 9 6
```

Time and again, the dangers of doubleton honour holdings have been illustrated and yet mistakes are still frequent in this area, even in the top-class game.

You should have realised that, once partner showed out on the second heart, South's third heart was premature. With the count now known, he should have played the ♣Q at once. Now, if you unblock, he returns to dummy with the remaining heart and leads towards his ♣9. If you fail to unblock, he now cashes the third heart and exits in clubs as before.

Hand No. 14

Dealer South
Neither vulnerable

W	N	E	S
			1♦
4♡	4♠	Dble	5♣
Dble	Redble	end	

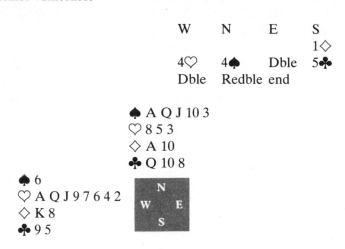

♠ A Q J 10 3
♡ 8 5 3
♢ A 10
♣ Q 10 8

♠ 6
♡ A Q J 9 7 6 4 2
♢ K 8
♣ 9 5

You lead the ♠6 to ace, four and five. Declarer draws trumps in three rounds, partner following with 6, 4 and 3 and then advances the ♠Q. Partner covers and South ruffs; plan your defence.

Partner's obviously low point-count and petering in trumps suggest a void of hearts and it looks as though you could have made life easier for yourselves by leading the ace and another heart. But that horse has bolted and you had better roll-call the hand in detail before you make another mistake. The spade and club distributions are clear and with five clubs, South must have at least five diamonds as he bid that suit first. That ties up with partner's heart void leaving South with ♡ K 10 in a 1–2–5–5 shape. Declarer has five top trump tricks, three in spades and you can see that, if he has the queen and jack in diamonds, he can set up three more in that suit without difficulty, conceding two heart tricks at the end. East must therefore be credited with at least the jack.

You can now see the danger. If South plays ace and another diamond, you will be in and forced to concede a heart trick. Yes, it's that dreaded doubleton honour again! Strangely, you have no less than four opportunities to stay out of trouble. Either discard the king now, play it on the first round of diamonds or discard it on one of dummy's spade winners which South will have to cash before exiting in diamonds.

The full deal:

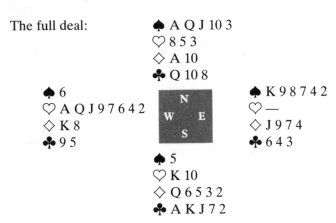

♠ A Q J 10 3
♡ 8 5 3
◇ A 10
♣ Q 10 8

♠ 6
♡ A Q J 9 7 6 4 2
◇ K 8
♣ 9 5

♠ K 9 8 7 4 2
♡ —
◇ J 9 7 4
♣ 6 4 3

♠ 5
♡ K 10
◇ Q 6 5 3 2
♣ A K J 7 2

When this hand came up, South provided West with a fifth chance by cashing his last trump before playing a diamond to the ace. The defender played the king on that first round of diamonds, thus taking the third of his five chances.

Hand No. 15

Dealer North
Neither vulnerable

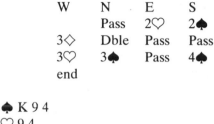

W	N	E	S
	Pass	2♡	2♠
3♢	Dble	Pass	Pass
3♡	3♠	Pass	4♠
end			

♠ K 9 4
♡ 9 4
♢ Q 9 5 4 2
♣ A 5 3

♠ A J 10 7 5
♡ A 3
♢ 10
♣ K J 10 9 4

East's opening bid showed 7–10 points and exactly six hearts to at least one of the top three honours.

West leads the ♡Q and East plays an encouraging ♡8 (remember the count is known). How do you play?

You will be losing one trick in each red suit so it seems to be a question of guessing one of the black queens. However, you can improve your chances slightly. You should have remarked on the fact that West bid diamonds but failed to lead them which strongly suggests that he does not hold both top honours. In that case, if the suit breaks 6–1, as is likely, East could be in trouble if you duck the first heart, win the likely continuation and exit in diamonds. If West ducks, East is endplayed and must give you a free finesse or ruff and discard. West will have to be very good to rise with the ♢A, crashing East's king and then lead another diamond. When you put in the nine, East must refuse to ruff and if you cash the ♢Q, he must refuse again. Even if your opponents are that good, the two finesses will still be available.

The full deal:

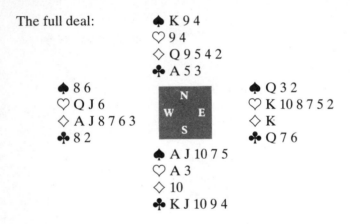

```
                    ♠ K 9 4
                    ♡ 9 4
                    ♢ Q 9 5 4 2
                    ♣ A 5 3
    ♠ 8 6                          ♠ Q 3 2
    ♡ Q J 6            N           ♡ K 10 8 7 5 2
    ♢ A J 8 7 6 3   W   E         ♢ K
    ♣ 8 2              S           ♣ Q 7 6
                    ♠ A J 10 7 5
                    ♡ A 3
                    ♢ 10
                    ♣ K J 10 9 4
```

Hand No. 16

Dealer East
E–W vulnerable

W	N	E	S
		Pass	1NT
Pass	2♣	Pass	2♡
Pass	3♡	Pass	4♡
end			

♠ K
♡ K J 10 4
♦ K J 9 5 4
♣ 10 6 4

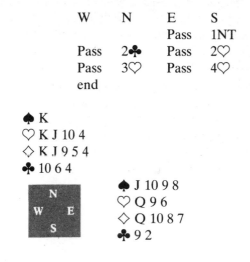

♠ J 10 9 8
♡ Q 9 6
♦ Q 10 8 7
♣ 9 2

South's opener showed 13–15 points and a Stayman sequence followed. Partner leads the queen, king and ace of clubs; plan your defence.

You can see that, if South can follow to the third club, a fourth round will promote a trump trick for you. If North fails to put in a high trump, you will play your nine and if he puts in an honour, you will discard, leaving yourself with an impregnable tenace. After petering on the first two rounds of clubs, the problem is how to tell him. It will be particularly difficult for him to realise what is required if he started with five clubs as he now knows he is giving a ruff and discard. Playing McKenney discards, it would be useful to discard a very low card in one of the other suits to indicate an interest in clubs. Sadly, you haven't got one. The best way to alert partner is to throw the ♢Q. This will clarify that you have no interest in making tricks in that suit. The ♢Q can hardly be interpreted as McKenney for spades. You would have ruffed the third club and cashed ♠A if you had held it. Thus it will be clear to partner that there is something else in the air.

The full deal:

```
                    ♠ K
                    ♡ K J 10 4
                    ◇ K J 9 5 4
                    ♣ 10 6 4
♠ 7 6 5 2                          ♠ J 10 9 8
♡ 7 2           N                 ♡ Q 9 6
◇ 6 3       W       E             ◇ Q 10 8 7
♣ A K Q 8 5     S                 ♣ 9 2
                    ♠ A Q 4 3
                    ♡ A 8 5 3
                    ◇ A 2
                    ♣ J 7 3
```

This spectacular discard of an honour to alert partner's attention is known as a 'foghorn' and where a queen is discarded, it is fitting that it should be called after a gentleman who discarded queens with remarkable regularity—the 'Henry the Eighth'. The discard most commonly occurs when East sits with a queen over dummy's king-jack and needs to tell his partner to go up with the ace, East knowing that this will be enough to beat the contract.

Here is an example:

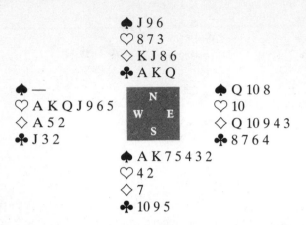

```
              ♠ J 9 6
              ♡ 8 7 3
              ◇ K J 8 6
              ♣ A K Q
♠ —                          ♠ Q 10 8
♡ A K Q J 9 6 5     N        ♡ 10
◇ A 5 2          W     E     ◇ Q 10 9 4 3
♣ J 3 2              S       ♣ 8 7 6 4
              ♠ A K 7 5 4 3 2
              ♡ 4 2
              ◇ 7
              ♣ 10 9 5
```

At love all, South opens 3♠, West bids 4♡ and North bids 4♠ to close the auction. West starts with heart honours and East can see that, once the second heart stands up, the contract will be beaten if West takes his ◇A. On the third heart, he discards the ◇Q. If he didn't, West, ignorant of the trump trick available to the defence, might play low on the first round of diamonds, thinking that the only hope rests in two diamond tricks.

Hand No. 17

Dealer East
Both vulnerable

W	N	E	S
		3◇	4♡
Pass	5◇	Pass	5♠
Pass	6◇	Pass	7♡
end			

♠ K 10 6 2
♡ A 10 2
◇ A
♣ 9 7 6 3 2

♠ A J
♡ K Q J 8 6 5
◇ J 8 7
♣ A J

You have been a little over-enthusiastic in the bidding on this hand but, inevitably, opponents' preempts leave relatively little room for lengthy discussions and bidding accuracy suffers.

West leads the ◇10; plan the play.

Counting tricks will give you a good guide to your possible options. There are six heart tricks on top, the minor aces and two top spades to total ten with the possibility of two diamond ruffs in dummy and a successful spade finesse or only one diamond ruff and four tricks in spades. If you are going to take two diamond ruffs in dummy, you will have to keep both dummy's high trumps available, otherwise, if the diamonds are 8–1, West could ruff in front of dummy twice, scoring the second time. Four spade tricks would imply the need for East to have the queen among not more than three and this is against the odds.

It best to establish the diamond position first. After winning the lead perforce in dummy, you should cross to the ♣A and lead a second diamond. If West ruffs in front of you, overruff, lead a spade to the ace and run the ♠J. If West covers, win and hope ♠10 stands up for the club discard. Then cross to hand with a trump, ruff the diamond, cross to hand by ruffing one of the black suits, according to how the spades have gone so far, draw trumps and claim. If West follows to the second diamond, you can ruff low in dummy and take a round of trumps. If East shows out, you cross to ♠A and run the jack as before. Now, it is certain that the ♠10 will stand up after which you can cross back to hand with a club ruff. (This is important if West has shown long spades, otherwise he will discard his second club on the ensuing diamond ruff to lock you in dummy.) Take the second diamond ruff, cross back with a black-suit ruff (chosen according to how the spades have broken so far), draw trumps and claim.

If West fails to cover the ♠J, he is only helping you because now you can take the second diamond ruff immediately, and even if that allows him to discard his second club, you can ruff your way back to hand in spades to draw the remaining trumps.

The full deal:

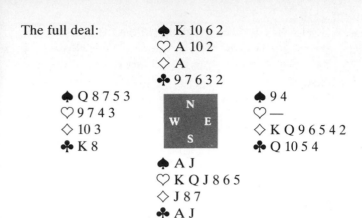

```
                    ♠ K 10 6 2
                    ♡ A 10 2
                    ◇ A
                    ♣ 9 7 6 3 2
   ♠ Q 8 7 5 3                        ♠ 9 4
   ♡ 9 7 4 3         N                ♡ —
   ◇ 10 3      W           E          ◇ K Q 9 6 5 4 2
   ♣ K 8             S                ♣ Q 10 5 4
                    ♠ A J
                    ♡ K Q J 8 6 5
                    ◇ J 8 7
                    ♣ A J
```

Hand No. 18

Dealer East
E–W vulnerable

W	N	E	S
		Pass	1◇
Pass	1♡	Pass	2♣
Pass	2♠	Pass	2NT
Pass	3♣	Pass	3♠
Pass	4◇	Pass	5♣
end			

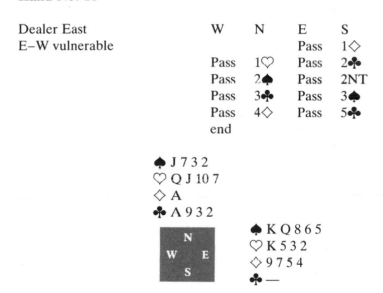

```
                    ♠ J 7 3 2
                    ♡ Q J 10 7
                    ◇ A
                    ♣ A 9 3 2
                         N
                    W         E    ♠ K Q 8 6 5
                         S         ♡ K 5 3 2
                                   ◇ 9 7 5 4
                                   ♣ —
```

By supporting the clubs after the fourth-suit-forcing two spade bid, North set up a forcing situation and cue-bidding followed.

Partner leads the ♠9 to the two, queen and ace. South crosses to the ◇A and calls for the ♠3; plan your defence.

Partner's lead is clearly from a doubleton and declarer is obviously trying to set up the ♣J for a heart discard, his distribution being 2–1–5–5. Clearly therefore, you must rise with the ♠K and attack hearts, but note it will not be good enough to lead a low one. You must consider where your third trick is coming from. It is likely that a trump promotion will be necessary and that implies the need for a further spade from your side. After rising with the ♠K, you should cash the ♡K and then revert to spades. Note that, even forgetting South's failure to cue-bid it, you can be confident that he does not hold the ♡A. If he had, he would have cashed it early and organised a ruffing finesse against your king for a spade discard.

The full deal:

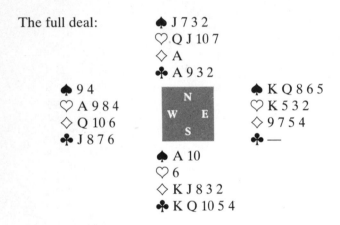

```
                    ♠ J 7 3 2
                    ♡ Q J 10 7
                    ◇ A
                    ♣ A 9 3 2
   ♠ 9 4                              ♠ K Q 8 6 5
   ♡ A 9 8 4          N               ♡ K 5 3 2
   ◇ Q 10 6      W         E          ◇ 9 7 5 4
   ♣ J 8 7 6          S               ♣ —
                    ♠ A 10
                    ♡ 6
                    ◇ K J 8 3 2
                    ♣ K Q 10 5 4
```

Observe what happens if you play a low heart—partner wins and a red card sets up two extra tricks for South immediately, so West must play a trump. South wins in hand, ruffs a diamond low, draws trumps and claims.

Hand No. 19

Dealer East
E–W vulnerable

W	N	E	S
		2◇	Dble
2♡	3♡	Pass	3♠
Pass	4♣	Pass	4◇
Pass	4♡	Pass	5♣
Pass	5◇	Pass	6◇
end			

♠ 7 3
♡ A 10 3
◇ A 8 2
♣ A J 10 9 2

♠ A Q J 9 6
♡ —
◇ K Q J 7 5
♣ Q 7 5

East's opening bid shows 11–15 points, a three-suited hand with a singleton or void diamond and no five-card major. Thus when West leads the ♣3, you can confidently place East with 4–4–1–4. How do you play?

Strong one club players are proud of the very accurate description of many of their systemic bids. On occasions, however, such assets can become liabilities, notably when the hand concerned fails to become dummy. Here you can place every card and form an accurate plan now, and, as you will see, it's just as well. You have five trump tricks, a heart, four clubs and three spades on the marked finesse, totalling twelve but there could be entry problems. You must obviously rise with the ♣A to avoid an immediate ruff and draw trumps (taking one spade finesse in dummy on the way) before continuing clubs. But on the second round, East can allow your queen to hold and you will be an entry short. If you play a low club second time, he wins and returns a third club, again cutting you off from dummy.

To avert this problem, you must use a rare form of Morton's Fork. Unblock the ♣Q on trick one, take two rounds of trumps in dummy and a spade finesse. The remaining trumps are drawn, and a low club to the nine puts East on the rack. If he wins, the whole suit comes in. If he holds up, you discard your last club on the ♡A, take a second spade finesse and give up one trick in that suit instead to make your hand high.

The full deal:

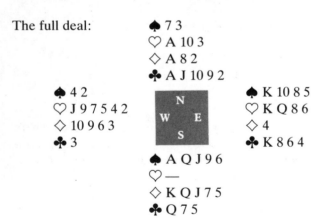

```
                ♠ 7 3
                ♡ A 10 3
                ◇ A 8 2
                ♣ A J 10 9 2
  ♠ 4 2                          ♠ K 10 8 5
  ♡ J 9 7 5 4 2      N           ♡ K Q 8 6
  ◇ 10 9 6 3     W       E       ◇ 4
  ♣ 3                S           ♣ K 8 6 4
                ♠ A Q J 9 6
                ♡ —
                ◇ K Q J 7 5
                ♣ Q 7 5
```

Hand No. 20

Dealer West
Both vulnerable

W	N	E	S
Pass	2NT	Pass	3♦
Pass	4♦	Dble	5♡
Pass	6♡	end	

♠ A Q 7
♡ A J 9 5
♦ A J
♣ A Q 5 4

♠ K J 10 6
♡ 8 2
♦ 10 9 8 5 4 3
♣ 2

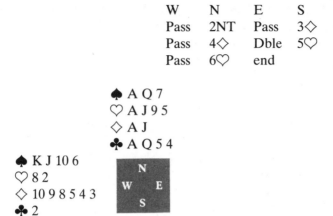

After North had promised 20–22, balanced, South transferred to hearts. North, with a maximum and good trump support cue-bids, showing the ace of diamonds and either both or neither of the two black aces.

Realistically thinking that you are unlikely to enjoy a club ruff and that leading one might damage partner's holding, you decide to respect his bidding and lead the ♦10 which goes to the ace, six and seven. All follow to the ace and king of trumps and now South leads the queen; plan your defence.

With South having promised a five-card heart suit in the bidding, you should realise that this third round of trumps has been played for no other reason than to invite you do something stupid. To avoid trouble, you must anticipate what is to follow. There is a danger that South may play one or two rounds of clubs, eliminate diamonds and then take the spade finesse and play two more rounds, leaving you on play in a layout like this:

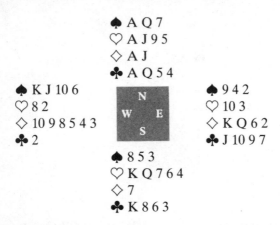

```
              ♠ A Q 7
              ♡ A J 9 5
              ◇ A J
              ♣ A Q 5 4
♠ K J 10 6                    ♠ 9 4 2
♡ 8 2            N            ♡ 10 3
◇ 10 9 8 5 4 3  W   E         ◇ K Q 6 2
♣ 2             S            ♣ J 10 9 7
              ♠ 8 5 3
              ♡ K Q 7 6 4
              ◇ 7
              ♣ K 8 6 3
```

Forced to concede a ruff and discard, you will present declarer with a hopeless contract. You must thus hang on to your ♣6 and be prepared to play honours on the first two rounds, giving your partner a chance to win the third round and exit safely in clubs. It is instructive to note that, if North is declarer and East leads the ♣J, the contract cannot fail. North draws trumps, eliminates the diamonds and now three rounds of spades leave the defender, who wins the third round, endplayed. Few bidding systems, however, put a value on the ♣8!

Hand No. 21

Dealer East
N–S vulnerable

W	N	E	S
		Pass	1♠
Pass	2♦	Pass	3♠
Pass	4♠	end	

♠ 8 4
♡ A 10 5 3
♦ A 9 6 3 2
♣ J 5

♠ A K Q 7 6 5
♡ Q
♦ 8 7 5
♣ A 9 2

West leads the ♡2; plan the play.

Counting tricks, you can see three side-suit aces and as the enemy have (just for once) been kind enough not to lead a trump, a ruff and six trump tricks in hand. Thus, as long as the trumps break 3–2, there should be no problem. You must thus address yourself to the possibility of a 4–1 split. This is another hand illustrating the importance of the play to the early tricks. Let us first consider trick one. In terms of total tricks, there is no risk in running the heart as you can always discard a losing diamond on the ♡A later. However, if East does produce the ♡K, he has a chance to return a trump to prevent the club ruff and may not be as generous as his partner! Having won the heart, you should aim to make your six trumps in hand by ruffing hearts, taking advantage of the likely 4–4 split, so that eventually, the enemy's two tricks in diamonds and one in trumps will coalesce into two. As entries are short in dummy, the process must start at once. Ruff a heart in hand at trick two and duck a club. Win any return and use dummy's ◇A and club ruff as entries to take two more heart ruffs. You will thus take ten tricks before the opponents have taken four.

The full deal:

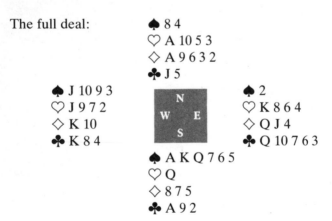

```
                    ♠ 8 4
                    ♡ A 10 5 3
                    ◇ A 9 6 3 2
                    ♣ J 5
  ♠ J 10 9 3                      ♠ 2
  ♡ J 9 7 2         N            ♡ K 8 6 4
  ◇ K 10        W       E        ◇ Q J 4
  ♣ K 8 4           S            ♣ Q 10 7 6 3
                    ♠ A K Q 7 6 5
                    ♡ Q
                    ◇ 8 7 5
                    ♣ A 9 2
```

Hand No. 22

Dealer West
N–S vulnerable

W	N	E	S
Pass	Pass	Pass	2NT
Pass	3NT	end	

♠ A 4
♡ 6 5
♢ 8 5 3
♣ Q 9 7 6 5 3

♠ K Q J 10
♡ K 4 3
♢ A K 9 6
♣ A J

West leads the ♡J to the five, eight and king. How do you continue?

After the lead, you have eight tricks on top and the ninth can only come from clubs. There are two possible lines: cross to dummy and take the finesse, risking defeat if it fails for lack of an entry to cash the queen, or bang down ace and jack from hand, ensuring an entry to the queen but now risking defeat if the hearts are 5–3 or worse. Is there any way to have your cake and eat it? As the best line depends on the heart distribution, that should be sought first as there is no rush to commit yourself to either line of play immediately. Simply return a heart. If the opponents cash out, you will know the distribution: if they are 4–4, you play clubs from the top; if they are 5–3, you will need the finesse.

The full deal:

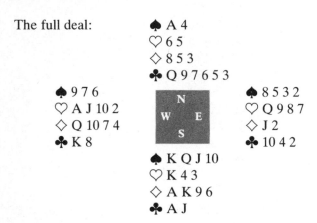

```
                    ♠ A 4
                    ♡ 6 5
                    ◇ 8 5 3
                    ♣ Q 9 7 6 5 3
  ♠ 9 7 6                              ♠ 8 5 3 2
  ♡ A J 10 2          N                ♡ Q 9 8 7
  ◇ Q 10 7 4      W       E            ◇ J 2
  ♣ K 8               S                ♣ 10 4 2
                    ♠ K Q J 10
                    ♡ K 4 3
                    ◇ A K 9 6
                    ♣ A J
```

Admittedly, you will look silly if the hearts are 6–2 or worse, but in the absence of a preempt or weak two, that is most unlikely on the bidding and even then, you will only have thrown the contract if the club finesse is right. Opponents might, of course, realise what is going on and refuse to cash, but you can always play on their nerves further with a third round on which the carding might indicate the position. At worst, you can always try one of the club lines and nothing will have been lost.

Hand No. 23

Dealer North
E–W vulnerable

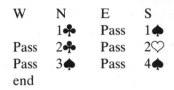

W	N	E	S
	1♣	Pass	1♠
Pass	2♣	Pass	2♡
Pass	3♠	Pass	4♠
end			

♠ Q 7 6
♡ 10
♢ J 8 7
♣ A K Q J 10 6

♠ 5 3
♡ A Q 6
♢ K Q 10 5
♣ 7 4 3 2

You lead the ♢K and it holds, partner playing the nine and declarer the two. How do you continue?

Your first duty here is to work out the meaning of partner's card. It could be encouraging, implying that he holds the ace. If he doesn't, he is signalling distribution—an even number. If it is four, you are most unlikely to defeat the contract (and in any case partner should not play his highest card to peter) so you should work on the assumption that it is a doubleton. That would leave South with four and therefore, on the bidding, a void in clubs and communication problems. It is thus clear that whether partner is encouraging or giving count, you must continue diamonds and you should realise that, provided partner has a top trump, you can keep declarer off the table by playing the $\diamondsuit$Q. You are thus assured of a third round ruff and provided that partner's trumps include the ace or king–jack, the contract is doomed. Note that there is no risk in crashing partner's $\diamondsuit$A—if he started with $\diamondsuit$Ax doubleton, he should overtake on trick one and return the suit, success being assured if you hold either major ace.

The full deal:

                     ♠ Q 7 6
                     ♡ 10
                     $\diamondsuit$ J 8 7
                     ♣ A K Q J 10 6

♠ 5 3
♡ A Q 6   ♠ A 8 4
$\diamondsuit$ K Q 10 5 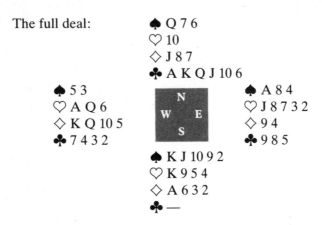 ♡ J 8 7 3 2
♣ 7 4 3 2 $\diamondsuit$ 9 4
                            ♣ 9 8 5

                     ♠ K J 10 9 2
                     ♡ K 9 5 4
                     $\diamondsuit$ A 6 3 2
                     ♣ —

Hand No. 24

Dealer South
E–W vulnerable

W	N	E	S
			1♡
Pass	1♠	Pass	3♡
Pass	4♢	Pass	4♠
Pass	4NT	Pass	5♣
Pass	6♡	end	

♠ A 5 3 2
♡ K Q 5 4
♢ A J
♣ 9 8 2

♠ K 7
♡ A J 10 7 6 2
♢ Q
♣ A 7 5 4

After your three heart bid, North's four diamonds was a cue-bid and according to your methods, you are allowed to show a king in partner's bid suit. Once cue-bidding has started, Blackwood does not apply and four no-trumps was simply a general slam try inviting you to cue-bid further.

West leads the ♣3 to East's ten; plan the play.

The diamond duplication means that you are in a poor contract and again you will have to allow yourself a lot of luck. Your six top heart tricks, two in spades and the two minor aces total ten so far and even if an endplay or squeeze is available, that is only likely to yield one extra trick. You must thus realise that the diamond finesse will have to be right and then try to dispose of one of your club losers. Players often complain when they lose contracts following bad distributions, but this is one occasion where you will need a 'bad' distribution (in clubs) if you are to have a chance.

You should assume that the hand with the short clubs (obviously West) has four or more spades. Win the first club, take the diamond finesse and draw two rounds of trumps, cashing the ◇A for a club discard on the way. Now the king and ace of spades are followed by a spade ruff in hand. Return to dummy in trumps to play a fourth spade for a second club discard. West wins and has to give you a ruff and discard and your last club disappears.

The full deal:

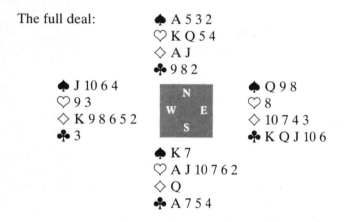

```
              ♠ A 5 3 2
              ♡ K Q 5 4
              ◇ A J
              ♣ 9 8 2
  ♠ J 10 6 4              ♠ Q 9 8
  ♡ 9 3          N        ♡ 8
  ◇ K 9 8 6 5 2  W   E    ◇ 10 7 4 3
  ♣ 3              S      ♣ K Q J 10 6
              ♠ K 7
              ♡ A J 10 7 6 2
              ◇ Q
              ♣ A 7 5 4
```

Note that the play to trick one virtually rules out a 4–2 club split and therefore a club-spade squeeze, and that the winning play would have been far more obvious if East had put in a club overcall.

Hand No. 25

Dealer South
Both vulnerable

W	N	E	S
			1♠
Pass	1NT	Dble	4♠
end			

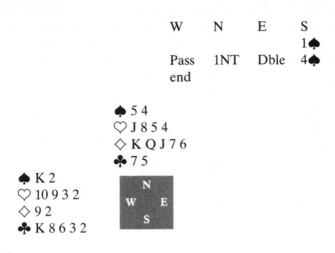

♠ 5 4
♡ J 8 5 4
♢ K Q J 7 6
♣ 7 5

♠ K 2
♡ 10 9 3 2
♢ 9 2
♣ K 8 6 3 2

You lead the ♢9 to the six, ace and ten. Partner returns the ♠7 and declarer puts in the queen; plan your defence.

A careful roll-call on the evidence so far will keep you on the right track. You should have noted a number of points. Firstly, partner immediately switched to trumps rather than attempt to cash top heart tricks. This implies that South has at least one of the heart honours. Secondly, partner seemed to be confident that South could not reach those diamonds on the table easily. This suggests that East started with five and knows the position. Third, partner entered the bidding, forcing you to the two-level, vulnerable, despite both opponents already having shown some strength and the probability that they have a misfit. The chances are that East has a singleton spade and now, all of a sudden, that pathetic little trump holding on dummy is loaded with gold. If you take your ♠K, South can overtake his ♠3 and enjoy the diamonds. Thus you must cash your tricks now and as the only hope lies in clubs, you should switch accordingly.

The full deal:

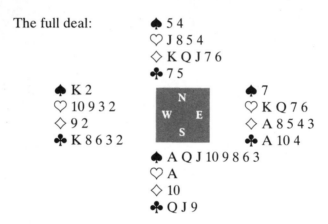

```
                    ♠ 5 4
                    ♡ J 8 5 4
                    ♢ K Q J 7 6
                    ♣ 7 5
  ♠ K 2                              ♠ 7
  ♡ 10 9 3 2          N             ♡ K Q 7 6
  ♢ 9 2          W         E        ♢ A 8 5 4 3
  ♣ K 8 6 3 2         S             ♣ A 10 4
                    ♠ A Q J 10 9 8 6 3
                    ♡ A
                    ♢ 10
                    ♣ Q J 9
```

You note that, if you decided to duck the trump trick, it is good enough as the cards lie. South will have to concede three club tricks as you can play your second trump when in with the ♣K. But it would not have been good enough had the positions of the ten and nine been exchanged!

Hand No. 26

Dealer North
Neither vulnerable

W	N	E	S
	Pass	Pass	1♠
2♠	Dble	2NT	Pass
3♣	Pass	Pass	3◇
Pass	4♠	end	

♠ J 5 3
♡ Q 7 5 4
◇ K 8 2
♣ A 10 5

♠ A 10 9 7 2
♡ A J
◇ A J 7 6 4
♣ 7

West's cue-bid showed at least 5–5 in hearts and a minor and after North's double, which suggested general values, East asked his partner to specify which minor.

West leads the ♣K to dummy's ace, East following with the three. You run the ♠J to West's king and ruff his return of the ♣Q, East playing the four. How do you continue?

You want to take finesses in both trumps and diamonds, but only have one entry to dummy. In situations like this, it pays to consider the consequences of alternative actions. If you try a second trump finesse and it succeeds, it will only be of value if the suit breaks 3–2. That implies that the diamonds will be 4–1 or worse and thus a near certainty that two tricks in the suit will have to be lost in addition to a heart and a trump.

There are advantages in preferring the diamond finesse. If it succeeds and West can follow, you know that he started with 1–5–2–5 and play the ♠10 to East whose best defence is to try to force you in clubs. You simply discard your losing heart to be able to take the next force in dummy and return to the ♡A, draw trumps and claim. If it succeeds and West ruffs low, you will be able to re-enter dummy with a fourth-round diamond ruff and take the trump finesse after all. If both diamonds and trumps are 4–1, you will ruff the fourth round of diamonds in dummy, take the trump finesse, cash the trump ace and then diamond winners, and the ♡A to keep control.

The full deal:

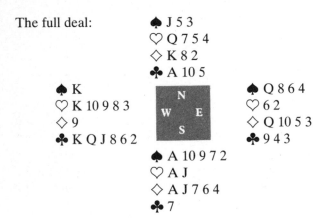

```
              ♠ J 5 3
              ♡ Q 7 5 4
              ◇ K 8 2
              ♣ A 10 5
♠ K                          ♠ Q 8 6 4
♡ K 10 9 8 3      N          ♡ 6 2
◇ 9          W       E       ◇ Q 10 5 3
♣ K Q J 8 6 2     S          ♣ 9 4 3
              ♠ A 10 9 7 2
              ♡ A J
              ◇ A J 7 6 4
              ♣ 7
```

Only if West turns up with exactly ◇ Q x, will this line fail.

Hand No. 27

Dealer East
E–W vulnerable

W	N	E	S
		Pass	1♣
Pass	1♢	Pass	1♠
Pass	2♡	Pass	2♠
Pass	3♡	Pass	3NT
Pass	5♣	end	

♠ —
♡ A K 8 5 4
♢ A 9 6 4 3 2
♣ 7 5

♠ K Q J 9
♡ Q J 10
♢ Q 10 8
♣ K 6 3

It is disconcerting that, when opponents have such an obviously wild distribution, everything seems to be breaking perfectly for them. However, this is the level of justice to which you are usually subjected and you decide to lead the ♡Q. Dummy wins, partner playing the two and South calls for the ♢A. All play low, but on the next round partner puts up the king and declarer ruffs with the ♣9; plan your defence.

It is obvious what is going to happen. The bidding and early play mark South with 5–2–1–5 and South is going to cash the ♠A and start ruffing spades. There will be enough entries for him to take three ruffs in his own hand after which he will exit in spades leaving himself with ♣ A Q and the defenders with nothing but trumps. Having already taken four top side-suit tricks and five ruffs, he will make the contract if East holds the ♣K or in this case, if you win trick ten. You must see to it that you do not by tossing in your three spade honours on the ace and the two ruffs in spades, hoping partner has the ten. Then he can win the last round and push a trump through.

The full deal:

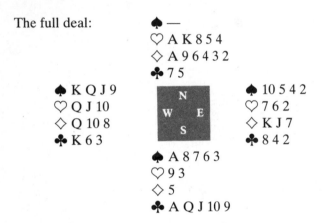

```
                    ♠ —
                    ♡ A K 8 5 4
                    ◇ A 9 6 4 3 2
                    ♣ 7 5
  ♠ K Q J 9                              ♠ 10 5 4 2
  ♡ Q J 10              N                ♡ 7 6 2
  ◇ Q 10 8          W       E            ◇ K J 7
  ♣ K 6 3              S                 ♣ 8 4 2
                    ♠ A 8 7 6 3
                    ♡ 9 3
                    ◇ 5
                    ♣ A Q J 10 9
```

A discussion about the bidding of this hand would require a chapter to itself, but you can muse on the facts that a trump lead does not defeat this contract, that a spade lead defeats three no-trumps and that four hearts is cold. Now, would partner have been astute enough to realise that a trump lead is needed to defeat five diamonds?

Hand No. 28

Dealer South
E–W vulnerable

W	N	E	S
			1♣
1♡	Pass	1♠	2♢
2♡	3♡	4♡	5♣
Pass	Pass	Dble	Pass
Pass	5♢	Dble	end

♠ 9 6 4
♡ A 7 2
♢ 10 5 3 2
♣ 10 8 7

♠ 8
♡ 3
♢ K Q 9 7 4
♣ A K J 9 4 3

After his early disciplined pass, your partner seems to have undergone a late rush of blood when he heard you reverse on your own.

West leads the ♣3 to his partner's ace and you ruff the return of the ♣Q. Trying to preserve the option of the club finesse, you decide to keep the ♡A in dummy and slip the ♢Q through. West, however, takes his ace and you have to ruff his return of the ♣K. How do you continue?

The bidding and early play have given you an accurate picture of the distribution. East must surely have started with six spades; yet his partner, despite holding K x x opposite, preferred to repeat his hearts. This can only be justified by a seven-card or longer suit. East's later support of hearts must promise at least a doubleton, confirming the 7–2 split. Thus West is 3–7–1–2 or 3–7–2–1. (If he is 7–3–3–0, your opponents are cold for at least 5♡ and would probably have bid on.) Which is it to be? The clue lies in the opening lead. With a singleton club, West could have ensured a set by leading it and then, on winning with the ace of trumps, putting his partner in with spades to receive a club ruff. Thus you should cross to dummy in hearts, take a trump finesse and hope that the clubs break 2–2.

The full deal:

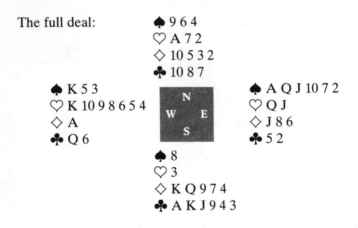

```
                    ♠ 9 6 4
                    ♡ A 7 2
                    ◇ 10 5 3 2
                    ♣ 10 8 7
♠ K 5 3                            ♠ A Q J 10 7 2
♡ K 10 9 8 6 5 4          N        ♡ Q J
◇ A                   W       E    ◇ J 8 6
♣ Q 6                     S        ♣ 5 2
                    ♠ 8
                    ♡ 3
                    ◇ K Q 9 7 4
                    ♣ A K J 9 4 3
```

Hand No. 29

Dealer West
Neither vulnerable

W	N	E	S
Pass	1NT	2♣	3♠
Pass	4♣	Pass	4♡
Pass	5♢	Pass	6♠
end			

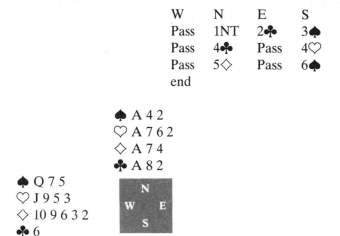

♠ A 4 2
♡ A 7 6 2
♢ A 7 4
♣ A 8 2

♠ Q 7 5
♡ J 9 5 3
♢ 10 9 6 3 2
♣ 6

North's opening bid showed 15–17 (picking up four aces, of course, only happens to other people!) and partner showed at least nine cards in hearts and a minor. After South's game-force, cue-bidding followed.

You lead your club to the two, ten and king. South returns the ♣4. It will clearly help declarer if you ruff so you discard a diamond and allow the ace to win, partner following with the three. Now declarer calls for a low heart from dummy and when partner puts up the queen, South ruffs; plan your defence.

This is a magic question classic and you will only have a chance to defeat this contract if you fully appreciate what is happening. South's early insistence on playing clubs clearly indicates that he is trying to set the suit up and that will involve giving a trick to partner and then enjoying a ruff in dummy. South appears to be 6–0–2–5 and any diamond loser can be discarded later on the ♡A. Now what was this heart ruff in hand all about? Why didn't he play a third club immediately? The reason is that, if he does, partner can play a fourth round at once and you can force dummy's ace of trumps to promote your queen. That means that he will have to slip one round of trumps past your queen before giving up the third club, after which the fourth club spells no danger. To prevent this, when South next plays a low spade honour, you must cover. Nothing now can prevent your side from taking a trump or extra club trick.

The full deal:

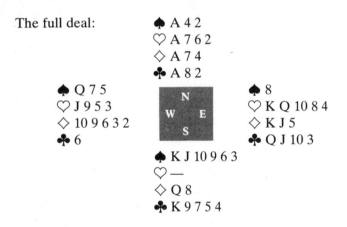

```
                    ♠ A 4 2
                    ♡ A 7 6 2
                    ♦ A 7 4
                    ♣ A 8 2
  ♠ Q 7 5                          ♠ 8
  ♡ J 9 5 3              N         ♡ K Q 10 8 4
  ♦ 10 9 6 3 2      W       E      ♦ K J 5
  ♣ 6                    S         ♣ Q J 10 3
                    ♠ K J 10 9 6 3
                    ♡ —
                    ♦ Q 8
                    ♣ K 9 7 5 4
```

South would, of course, have given you a harder problem if he had played the nine of spades at trick two.

Hand No. 30

Dealer West
E–W vulnerable

W	N	E	S
1NT	Pass	2♦	2♡
3♦	3♡	3♠	4♡
4♣	Pass	Pass	5♡
Dble	end		

```
              ♠ K 6 3
              ♡ J 10 7 3
              ♦ Q J 4
              ♣ A 8 2
♠ A 7 2
♡ A 8
♦ A 10 9 6
♣ Q J 9 7
```

Your opening bid showed 13–15 and partner made a natural weak take-out.

You lead the ♦A and regret it when South ruffs. He now plays the ♡K to your ace, partner discarding the ♣J. How do you continue?

You can thank your partner for this most revealing discard as it enables you to roll-call the hand almost exactly. Let us run through the list. You know that South has seven hearts, no diamonds and the ♠Q. Partner started with six diamonds and if he had held six spades as well, he surely would have bid them first. Equally, he would hardly have come in on a four-card suit, jack-high, on a hand of poor point-count at this vulnerability— so he must have five. That leaves South with four clubs, surely to the king, as shown here:

The full deal:

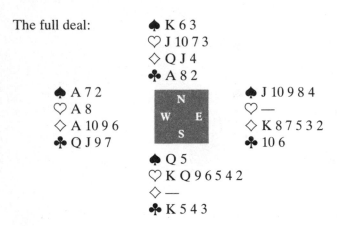

This gives South six trump tricks, one spade and two top clubs to total nine so far and a ruffing finesse against partner in diamonds will set up a tenth. He could theoretically ruff his fourth club in dummy, but that implies giving up a trick initially, allowing three for the defence first. His only chance, therefore, lies in Morton's Fork. Suppose you exit passively in trumps or clubs; South would win and push a low spade through your hand. If you win, you concede an extra spade trick. If not, declarer takes a ruffing finesse in diamonds for a spade discard and now can, after all, afford to concede a club.

To counter this, you must force South to use this discard prematurely. You should play the ◇10 now and hope partner realises that he must not cover, forcing South to discard too early. If he throws a spade, you can take his queen and wait for a club trick. If he throws a club, you will duck the spade and the queen can no longer be discarded so you still have a trick in each black suit to come.

You should have realised that South misplayed the hand. A spade at trick two would have punished your error on the opening lead.

Hand No. 31

Dealer East
N–S vulnerable

W	N	E	S
		1NT	Pass
2♡	Dble	2♠	3♠
Pass	4♣	Pass	4♡
Pass	5♡	Pass	6♡
end			

♠ 9
♡ A J 7 5
♢ A K 6 3
♣ A J 7 6

♠ A 8 4
♡ K Q 9 4
♢ 8 2
♣ Q 10 4 3

After East's 12–14 no-trump, West transferred to spades and after partner indicated hearts and East showed some interest in spades, you made an advance cue-bid in support of hearts.

West leads the ♣2; plan the play.

All the points are marked in the East hand so the club finesse must fail and the lead, particularly after East had indicated his spade holding, has all the hallmarks of a singleton. You have three club tricks and three other tops in the side-suits, but if you try to take six trump tricks, either by ruffing two spades on dummy or two diamonds in hand, you will have communication problems. You cannot cross in clubs and if you ruff spades and cross with a diamond ruff or vice versa, then by the time you have completed drawing trumps, you will have none left. When you give up the ♣K, the defenders will cash all their spades.

Bearing in mind that West is threatening the ruff, you have to appreciate that, if his trumps are as good as 10 x x the contract cannot be made, but it is cold if he has a doubleton or three small. Win the lead in dummy, cash the ♠A and take a spade ruff in dummy. Now play a trump to the queen and take a second ruff with the ace of trumps. Now play the ♡J; if East plays the ten, overtake, draw the last trump and give up a club. If East plays low, so does South after which you give up a club immediately.

The full deal:

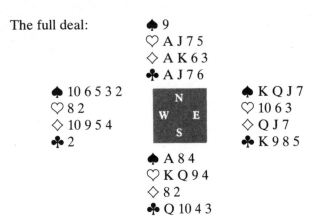

```
                    ♠ 9
                    ♡ A J 7 5
                    ♢ A K 6 3
                    ♣ A J 7 6
  ♠ 10 6 5 3 2                      ♠ K Q J 7
  ♡ 8 2              N              ♡ 10 6 3
  ♢ 10 9 5 4    W       E          ♢ Q J 7
  ♣ 2              S                ♣ K 9 8 5
                    ♠ A 8 4
                    ♡ K Q 9 4
                    ♢ 8 2
                    ♣ Q 10 4 3
```

Hand No. 32

Dealer West
N–S vulnerable

W	N	E	S
Pass	2♣	Pass	2♡
Pass	3♢	Pass	4♣
Pass	4♡	Pass	5♣
Pass	5NT	Pass	7♡
end			

♠ A K 8
♡ A J 7
♢ A K Q 8 6 3
♣ 9

♠ 5
♡ K Q 6 4 3
♢ 5 4
♣ A Q 7 6 2

After hearts were agreed, your five clubs was a cue-bid and five no-trumps asked for two of the top three trump honours for a grand slam.

West leads the ♣J; plan the play.

The premature removal of your spade entry has prevented you from coping with a 4–1 split in both red suits, but you can handle a bad break in either if you test trumps first. Play two rounds, leaving a high honour in dummy. If a defender shows out, cash the third trump, return to hand with the ♣A to draw the last trump and hope for 3–2 break in diamonds.

If both defenders follow to two rounds of trumps, you can cash the ◇A, discard your second diamond on the ♠A and ruff a diamond high in hand. Then return to dummy in trumps, drawing the last one in the process, to cash the rest of the diamonds.

The full deal:

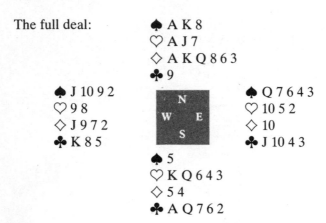

```
                    ♠ A K 8
                    ♡ A J 7
                    ◇ A K Q 8 6 3
                    ♣ 9
    ♠ J 10 9 2                      ♠ Q 7 6 4 3
    ♡ 9 8            N              ♡ 10 5 2
    ◇ J 9 7 2     W   E            ◇ 10
    ♣ K 8 5          S             ♣ J 10 4 3
                    ♠ 5
                    ♡ K Q 6 4 3
                    ◇ 5 4
                    ♣ A Q 7 6 2
```

The alternative line of ruffing two clubs in dummy will fail if the trumps break 4–1 or if West has five or more clubs and East the ♡10.

Hand No. 33

Dealer South
N–S vulnerable

W	N	E	S
			1♣
Pass	1♡	Pass	1♠
Pass	2♢	Pass	4♣
Pass	6♣	end	

♠ 8 5
♡ K J 9 5 2
♢ A Q 5 2
♣ 10 9

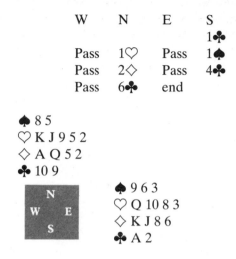

♠ 9 6 3
♡ Q 10 8 3
♢ K J 8 6
♣ A 2

After North's fourth-suit forcing two diamonds, South indicated a strong six-card or longer club suit.

Partner leads the ♡6 to the two, eight and ace. South cashes the two top spades, partner following with the four and two, and ruffs a third round in dummy, partner playing the ten. Now follows the ♡K from dummy on which South throws the ♢4 and the ♢A to the six, seven and three. Declarer then ruffs a diamond in hand and leads the ♠J, covered by the queen and ruffed in dummy; plan your defence.

Declarer is obviously 4–1–2–6 and the only hope for the defence seems to lie in a second trump trick. But this seems impossible as West still has one card in each red suit. Overruffing allows South to ruff any return low and draw trumps. If you discard a red card, South will return to hand in that suit and lead a high trump. When you win with the ace, you will have to return the other red suit which South will be able to ruff low while West still has to follow. This point gives the clue to a possible winning solution— try the effect of underruffing. Now, whichever suit South uses to return to hand, you will still have a card in it to lead after the trump ace and if your partner has the ♣8, that will be enough.

The full deal:

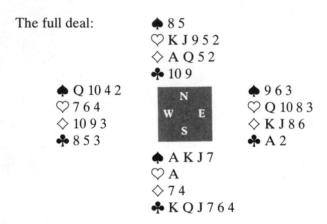

```
                    ♠ 8 5
                    ♡ K J 9 5 2
                    ◇ A Q 5 2
                    ♣ 10 9
  ♠ Q 10 4 2                        ♠ 9 6 3
  ♡ 7 6 4          N                ♡ Q 10 8 3
  ◇ 10 9 3       W   E              ◇ K J 8 6
  ♣ 8 5 3          S                ♣ A 2
                    ♠ A K J 7
                    ♡ A
                    ◇ 7 4
                    ♣ K Q J 7 6 4
```

Declarer can still get home if he ruffs his way back to hand and leads a low trump, but he risks looking very silly if you have underruffed with two low cards. This position is a rare variation of what Kelsey and Ottlik described in *Adventures in Card Play* as a 'backwash squeeze'—East is squeezed in three suits including trumps. The first recorded example was (coincidentally also a six club contract) played by the Australian, Tim Seres, some years ago.

Hand No. 34

Dealer East
Both vulnerable

W	N	E	S
		Pass	1♠
Pass	2♣	Pass	2◇
Pass	2♡	Pass	4♣
Pass	4♡	Pass	4NT
Pass	6♠	end	

♠ A 8 7 2
♡ A 9
◇ 5 3 2
♣ K J 10 3

♠ Q 10 9 6 4
♡ 6
◇ A K 8 6
♣ A Q 4

This is an awkward hand to bid. After North's fourth-suit forcing two hearts, you were too strongly merely to bid three clubs. North's four hearts was a cue-bid (on the basis that clubs was the agreed suit although he knew he was going to correct any club contract to spades). Once cue-bidding has started, Blackwood does not apply. Your 4NT was a general slam try and, in this situation, denied the ♣A and therefore strongly implied the ◇A. Note that to bid five diamonds (admittedly clearer) commits the partnership to six clubs and thereby implies an interest in a grand slam.

West leads the ♡Q; plan the play.

It appears that a diamond trick will have to be lost so it looks like a question of avoiding a trump loser. There are thus two possible lines: cash the ace hoping to drop a singleton king with West or run the queen, hoping to pin a singleton jack with East. The two have an equal chance and with nothing else to go on, running the queen is the slightly better bet. Many defenders holding K x may feel that their king is caught and that the only chance is to duck smoothly, hoping you have longer spades and may play for the drop.

However, in this hand, the ace is the superior play because all is not lost if the singleton king is with East.

The full deal:

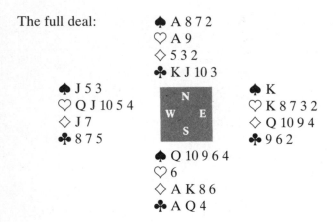

```
                    ♠ A 8 7 2
                    ♡ A 9
                    ♢ 5 3 2
                    ♣ K J 10 3
  ♠ J 5 3                          ♠ K
  ♡ Q J 10 5 4         N           ♡ K 8 7 3 2
  ♢ J 7            W       E       ♢ Q 10 9 4
  ♣ 8 7 5              S           ♣ 9 6 2
                    ♠ Q 10 9 6 4
                    ♡ 6
                    ♢ A K 8 6
                    ♣ A Q 4
```

Now, if West has two or fewer diamonds, you can get home by ruffing the ♡9, cashing the ♠Q and the two top diamonds and playing on clubs. If West ruffs, he will have to concede a ruff and discard. If he doesn't, you will throw him in with a third round of trumps for a similar conclusion.

Hand No. 35

Dealer South
Neither vulnerable

W	N	E	S
			1NT
Pass	2NT	Pass	3NT
end			

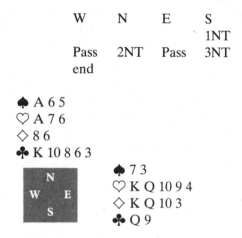

♠ A 6 5
♡ A 7 6
♢ 8 6
♣ K 10 8 6 3

♠ 7 3
♡ K Q 10 9 4
♢ K Q 10 3
♣ Q 9

South's opening bid showed 12–14 and he is clearly good in that range.

Partner gets off to his usual dazzling start by leading the ♠J. South's queen wins and he cashes the ♣A and follows with the ♣4. Partner follows with the two and the five. How do you visualise the defence and would it make any difference if partner's first two clubs are the two and the seven?

This is another beautiful exercise in roll-calling, particularly so as it all has to be done at trick one. Let us first consider points. You can see twenty-three and with South having promised at least thirteen, partner can have four at most and he has already shown the ♠J. If his other honour is the ♠K, there is no hope—South will make two spade tricks, four clubs, two in diamonds and a heart. So the ♠K must be credited to South. It appears from the way that he is tackling the clubs, that South lacks the jack, so partner will have the two black jacks plus one or both of the other two jacks. Now let us count the clubs. If South has three, he has four club tricks, three spades and two red aces—no hope. Thus South must be given a doubleton. Note that West does not peter with his four-card suit—that is more likely to help declarer. Now, if South cashes the top two clubs, dummy's 10 8 will then be equals against partner's J 7 and again the contract is unbeatable. The way to deflect declarer from this path is to throw the queen on the first round. This virtually obliges declarer to play a 'safe' eight on the second round. Your nine wins and now you have a chance provided that you do not switch to a red suit where South has the jack. Partner's ♣5 suggest a diamond; the ♣7 would suggest a heart, but at the risk of forgoing extra undertricks, it is probably safest to play your other spade.

The full deal:

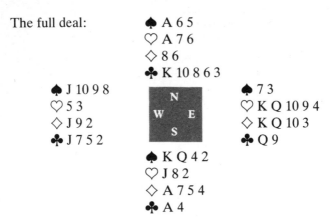

```
                    ♠ A 6 5
                    ♡ A 7 6
                    ◇ 8 6
                    ♣ K 10 8 6 3
  ♠ J 10 9 8              N          ♠ 7 3
  ♡ 5 3              W         E     ♡ K Q 10 9 4
  ◇ J 9 2                             ◇ K Q 10 3
  ♣ J 7 5 2               S          ♣ Q 9
                    ♠ K Q 4 2
                    ♡ J 8 2
                    ◇ A 7 5 4
                    ♣ A 4
```

Hand No. 36

Dealer East
Neither vulnerable

W	N	E	S
		Pass	1♠
Pass	2♣	Pass	3♡
Pass	3NT	Pass	4♠
Pass	5♣	Pass	6♠
end			

♠ 8 7 2
♡ 6 4 2
◇ A Q 10
♣ A 7 5 2

♠ A K 9 6 4 3
♡ A K Q J
◇ 9 4 2
♣ —

West leads the ♣J; plan the play.

There will be no problem if the trumps break evenly or if the diamond finesse works. You also have chances to cater for East having the long trumps and the ◇K provided you take necessary precautions early. Win the club in dummy, discarding a diamond, and ruff a club immediately. Now two top trumps see West show out and you cash the hearts, ruffing the last round in order to ruff a further club. Now exit in trumps and you may find that East has nothing left in his hand but diamonds.

The full deal:

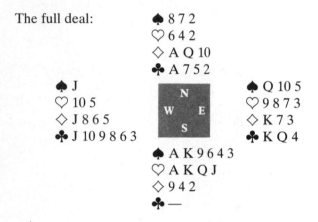

```
                    ♠ 8 7 2
                    ♡ 6 4 2
                    ◇ A Q 10
                    ♣ A 7 5 2
    ♠ J                              ♠ Q 10 5
    ♡ 10 5             N             ♡ 9 8 7 3
    ◇ J 8 6 5      W       E         ◇ K 7 3
    ♣ J 10 9 8 6 3     S             ♣ K Q 4
                    ♠ A K 9 6 4 3
                    ♡ A K Q J
                    ◇ 9 4 2
                    ♣ —
```

If East interrupts proceedings at any stage, the diamond finesse is always available. An initial diamond lead, of course, would have beaten you outright.

Hand No. 37

Dealer East
Both vulnerable

W	N	E	S
		Pass	1NT
2♠	Dble	Pass	4♡
end			

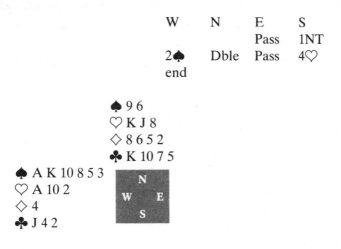

```
              ♠ 9 6
              ♡ K J 8
              ◇ 8 6 5 2
              ♣ K 10 7 5
♠ A K 10 8 5 3    N
♡ A 10 2        W   E
◇ 4               S
♣ J 4 2
```

South's opening bid showed 15–17 and denied a five-card major. North's double was competitive.

You cash your two spade tricks, partner following with the two and jack and South with the seven and queen. How do you plan the defence?

Partner's carding indicates a three-card holding with preference for diamonds rather than clubs. South will need the ♡Q and ♣ A Q if he is to have any chance at all. With the ♠Q already shown, that accounts for ten of his points and he must surely be maximum for his bid so he has seven points in diamonds and any diamond honour in partner's hand, probably the king, is badly placed. Opponents are playing a 4–3 fit and it is clear that your only hope for a fourth lies in trumps. You should therefore attack declarer's trumps by continuing spades.

But that is only the beginning. In situations like this, you must be careful to time your playing of the trump ace. If South ruffs in the short hand and leads a trump, you can rise with the ace on the first or second round and play a fourth spade. South will be forced to ruff in hand but if partner has the nine of trumps, he can put it in to force the queen, setting up your ten.

So South must ruff the third spade in the long hand and now the defence has to be even more meticulous. South starts drawing trumps and you must refuse two rounds, allowing him to take two diamond finesses. He can then cash the ♢A—you must refuse to ruff. When he plays on clubs, partner can ruff the third round. Any other defence lets the contract through.

The full deal:

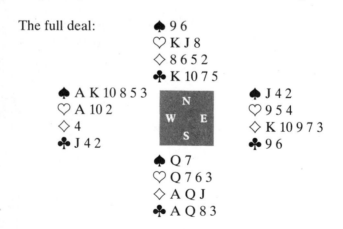

```
                    ♠ 9 6
                    ♡ K J 8
                    ♢ 8 6 5 2
                    ♣ K 10 7 5
♠ A K 10 8 5 3              ♠ J 4 2
♡ A 10 2        N          ♡ 9 5 4
♢ 4         W       E      ♢ K 10 9 7 3
♣ J 4 2          S         ♣ 9 6
                    ♠ Q 7
                    ♡ Q 7 6 3
                    ♢ A Q J
                    ♣ A Q 8 3
```

Hand No. 38

Dealer West
E–W vulnerable

W	N	E	S
2♡	Pass	2NT	3♠
Pass	Pass	4♡	Pass
Pass	4♠	end	

♠ 10 2
♡ 4 2
♢ K 10 9 4
♣ Q 10 9 8 6

♠ A Q 8 6 4 3
♡ 5
♢ A Q J 8
♣ K J

West's opening bid promised 8–11 points and exactly six hearts to at least one of the top three honours and East's response asked for further information regarding strength and suit quality within that range.

West leads the ♡K and on seeing an encouraging seven from his partner, continues with the queen which you have to ruff. How do you continue?

Success will depend on the way you play the trump suit and your first duty is to seek a more accurate points roll-call by smoking out the ♣A. If West has it, nine of his points are accounted for and you will take a simple trump finesse through East. But if East has it, then the ♠K is likely to be with West, in which case you should lay down the trump ace. If they both play low, it is better to play a low trump on the second round as West, with the longer hearts, is more likely to have the spade shortage.

If the king drops, you must cash two high diamonds, cross the dummy and play club winners through East, discarding diamonds, and then play dummy's diamonds. If East ruffs at any stage, you will overruff and concede only one trump trick. If East refuses to ruff, you will ruff dummy's last diamond winner perforce and exit with a low trump to the ten and jack, forcing East to lead away from his 9 7 to your Q 8 at trick twelve.

The full deal:

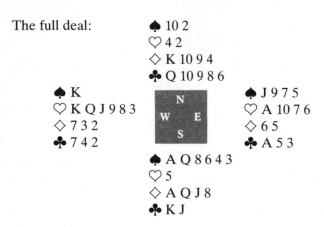

```
                  ♠ 10 2
                  ♡ 4 2
                  ◇ K 10 9 4
                  ♣ Q 10 9 8 6
♠ K                               ♠ J 9 7 5
♡ K Q J 9 8 3        N            ♡ A 10 7 6
◇ 7 3 2          W       E        ◇ 6 5
♣ 7 4 2              S            ♣ A 5 3
                  ♠ A Q 8 6 4 3
                  ♡ 5
                  ◇ A Q J 8
                  ♣ K J
```

Hand No. 39

Dealer South
E–W vulnerable

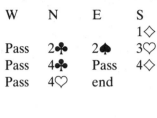

W	N	E	S
			1♢
Pass	2♣	2♠	3♡
Pass	4♣	Pass	4♢
Pass	4♡	end	

♠ J 7
♡ K 8 3
♢ 3
♣ A J 10 9 8 4 3

♠ 9 8 5 3
♡ J 7 6 5
♢ Q 7 6
♣ Q 7

You lead the ♠9 and partner wins with the king, South dropping the queen. When partner continues with the ace, South discards a diamond and partner persists with a third round of spades. South discards another diamond and ruffs in dummy. He now cashes two top diamonds, partner following with the nine and jack, and ruffs a third round with the ♡8, partner discarding a spade. Now follow the ♣A, a club ruff with the ♡9 and the ♢10; plan your defence.

This hand is another illustration of the importance of attacking declarer's trump holding when he is playing in a 4–3 fit. However, you must be careful not be caught with too many trumps. Suppose you throw off your last spade. Dummy ruffs and another club is ruffed high in hand, forcing you to underruff. Now the fifth diamond is ruffed in your hand and with partner unable to overruff, you are left on play and forced to lead into the trump tenace. To avoid this you must ruff the ◇10 and still underruff on the next club. On the fifth diamond, you will discard your spade, allowing partner to win and push a black card through South's trump tenace.

The full deal:

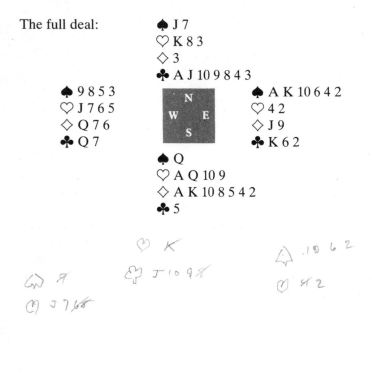

```
                    ♠ J 7
                    ♡ K 8 3
                    ◇ 3
                    ♣ A J 10 9 8 4 3
  ♠ 9 8 5 3                          ♠ A K 10 6 4 2
  ♡ J 7 6 5         N                ♡ 4 2
  ◇ Q 7 6        W     E             ◇ J 9
  ♣ Q 7            S                 ♣ K 6 2
                    ♠ Q
                    ♡ A Q 10 9
                    ◇ A K 10 8 5 4 2
                    ♣ 5
```

Hand No. 40

Dealer West
Both vulnerable

W	N	E	S
4♡	Dble	Pass	6♠
end			

♠ K Q 10 3 2
♡ 5
♢ A J 9
♣ K 9 8 6

♠ A J 8 6 5
♡ A 6 2
♢ 10 6 4
♣ A J

Partner's double was for take-out.
   West leads the ♢2; plan the play.

To open at game level, vulnerable, West must surely have tremendous hearts and yet he has chosen to lead a diamond. The lead has all the hallmarks of a singleton and this is another example of the advantage of a suit breaking badly and the consequent inability of the defenders to communicate. You should win the diamond, draw trumps in two rounds, cash the ace and king of clubs and ruff a third club in hand. Then cash the ♡A and ruff a heart before ruffing your last club in hand. Now play a third heart on which you discard a diamond from dummy, allowing West to hold the trick. Forced to lead another heart, he will have to give you a ruff and discard.

If trumps are 3–0, East having the length, you cannot play the same way because East will ruff the third heart and cash a diamond. In that case, and also if West has the length, the club finesse will be needed. (In the latter case, it is a near certainty.)

The full deal:

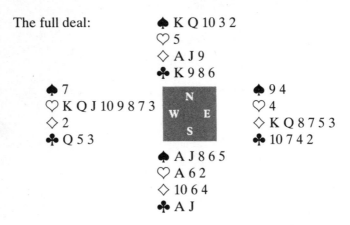

```
                    ♠ K Q 10 3 2
                    ♡ 5
                    ◇ A J 9
                    ♣ K 9 8 6
  ♠ 7                                    ♠ 9 4
  ♡ K Q J 10 9 8 7 3      N             ♡ 4
  ◇ 2                  W       E         ◇ K Q 8 7 5 3
  ♣ Q 5 3                 S             ♣ 10 7 4 2
                    ♠ A J 8 6 5
                    ♡ A 6 2
                    ◇ 10 6 4
                    ♣ A J
```

Hand No. 41

Dealer West
E–W vulnerable

W	N	E	S
1♣	Pass	Pass	1NT
Pass	2♣	Pass	2◇
Pass	3NT	end	

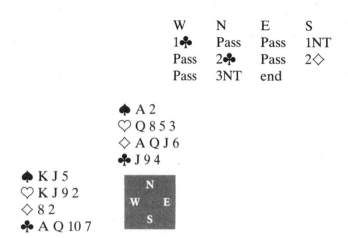

```
              ♠ A 2
              ♡ Q 8 5 3
              ◇ A Q J 6
              ♣ J 9 4
  ♠ K J 5        N
  ♡ K J 9 2   W     E
  ◇ 8 2          S
  ♣ A Q 10 7
```

Playing a variable no-trump, you open one club and South's one no-trump in the protective position showed about 12–14 points. Following a Stayman enquiry, North bid game.

Let us first consider the opening lead. It is clear that, with fourteen points in your hand and the opponents in game, your partner is going to make his usual massive contribution to the proceedings and you seem to be caught between the devil and the deep blue sea. A diamond lead is unlikely to give much away, but declarer is bound to continue the suit and you will have the pleasant task of deciding how you are going to be endplayed and/ or squeezed. It is probably better, therefore, to go on the attack and you lead the ♡2. This runs to the three, partner's ten and South's ace, and back comes the suit as South returns the seven; plan your defence.

You can set up a second heart trick for yourself by winning and playing a further round, but first consider the aftermath. Declarer can play four rounds of diamonds, forcing you to discard twice and you will have to give up your heart trick or present him with an extra trick in one of the black suits. Is there any other hope? Count declarer's tricks: two in hearts, four in diamonds and the ♠A make seven which means he will have to get the clubs going, involving surrendering the lead twice more. Therein lies your chance—in spades. If partner can manage just the ten, you can rise with the ♡K and play the ♠J now, the king next time and the five on the third round. Meanwhile you can safely discard two low clubs on the diamonds.

The full deal:

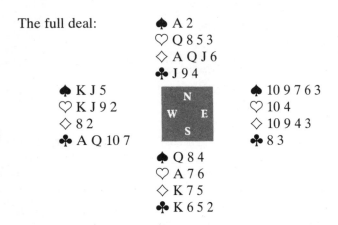

```
                       ♠ A 2
                       ♡ Q 8 5 3
                       ◇ A Q J 6
                       ♣ J 9 4
        ♠ K J 5                        ♠ 10 9 7 6 3
        ♡ K J 9 2          N           ♡ 10 4
        ◇ 8 2          W       E       ◇ 10 9 4 3
        ♣ A Q 10 7         S           ♣ 8 3
                       ♠ Q 8 4
                       ♡ A 7 6
                       ◇ K 7 5
                       ♣ K 6 5 2
```

If South now plays on clubs he will be twice down with partner's zero-count contributing no less than three tricks (you thought I was joking, didn't you?). Declarer can, of course, counter by rising with the ♠A, putting East out of the game. However, he is now short of entries to lead up to the ♣J twice and if he tries four round of diamonds and queen and another heart, you discard two clubs and exit with king and another spade to leave South with only eight tricks, and your two clubs are still to come.

Hand No. 42

Dealer East
E–W vulnerable

	W	N	E	S
			Pass	1NT
	Pass	6NT	end	

♠ A 2
♡ K 4 2
◇ A K 8 3
♣ A Q 7 5

```
      N
   W     E
      S
```

♠ K 5 3
♡ A Q 5
◇ 10 7 6 5
♣ K J 9

Your opening bid showed 12–14 points.

West leads the ♠Q which you win. On the first round of diamonds, West discards the ♡6. How do you play?

You are gratified that you stayed out of an impossible six diamonds (the ruffing value being worthless as you can discard the losing spade on clubs). Now your twelfth trick can only come from an endplay which means that East will have to be stripped down to nothing but diamonds. On the run of the clubs and hearts, he can release one diamond, but will have to come down to three diamonds and one spade (otherwise you set up a diamond). Now it is safe to cash your second spade before leading a low diamond from the table towards the ten and endplaying East.

The full deal:

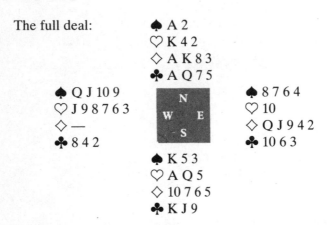

```
                    ♠ A 2
                    ♡ K 4 2
                    ◇ A K 8 3
                    ♣ A Q 7 5
♠ Q J 10 9                          ♠ 8 7 6 4
♡ J 9 8 7 6 3         N             ♡ 10
◇ —              W         E         ◇ Q J 9 4 2
♣ 8 4 2              S              ♣ 10 6 3
                    ♠ K 5 3
                    ♡ A Q 5
                    ◇ 10 7 6 5
                    ♣ K J 9
```

You did, of course, anticipate this and win the first spade in hand. If you did not, you are now stuck in the wrong hand and must concede defeat. Note that, if West has the diamond stack, there is little chance on this lead, but in that case he probably would have led one himself, anyway, after which the play is easy.

Hand No. 43

Dealer West
N–S vulnerable

W	N	E	S
2♡	2NT	Pass	3♠
Pass	4♠	end	

♠ K 7 4
♡ K 8 7 3
♢ K 10 3
♣ A K J

♠ A 9 8 6 2
♡ 4 2
♢ 8 7
♣ Q 7 6 5

At this vulnerability, West's opening bid showed 6–9 points with exactly six hearts to at least one of the top three honours.

West leads the ♡Q. You judge that it is unlikely that he would lead from the ace and play low in dummy. East takes his ace and returns the ♣10. How do you play?

Given a 3–2 break, you will have to lose one trump trick and the two red aces so it appears that all hangs on the position of the $\diamondsuit$A. However, there are two important points. Firstly, it is a near certainty that this ace is with East. Were it not, East could have returned a diamond and ruffed dummy's $\heartsuit$K. Admittedly that would not necessarily have spelt defeat as it might be his trump trick anyway, but he is unlikely to have wanted to lead round to dummy's club tenace if he did not hold the $\diamondsuit$A.

This hand illustrates again the importance of trying alternatives before banking on a finesse which can always wait. Win the club on dummy with the ace or king and take two top trumps. Now try to exhaust East of clubs by continuing the suit, overtaking the third round to ruff the fourth in dummy before exiting in trumps. East may be left with nothing but diamonds.

The full deal:

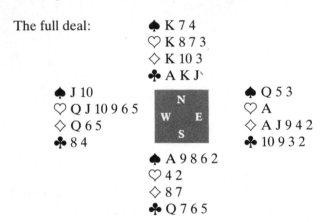

```
                    ♠ K 7 4
                    ♡ K 8 7 3
                    ◇ K 10 3
                    ♣ A K J
    ♠ J 10                          ♠ Q 5 3
    ♡ Q J 10 9 6 5      N           ♡ A
    ◇ Q 6 5        W       E        ◇ A J 9 4 2
    ♣ 8 4              S            ♣ 10 9 3 2
                    ♠ A 9 8 6 2
                    ♡ 4 2
                    ◇ 8 7
                    ♣ Q 7 6 5
```

Should he produce a fifth club, or if West has the third trump, the chance of a diamond to the king is still there. Note: if you try to allow dummy's third club to hold, you cannot get back to hand with the king and another heart. East will ruff in and exit with the fourth club, leaving you to play the diamonds.

Hand No. 44

Dealer East
E–W vulnerable

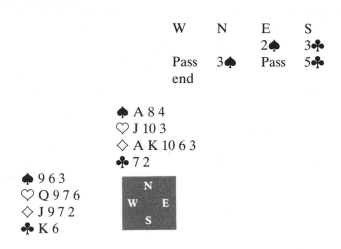

	W	N	E	S
			2♠	3♣
	Pass	3♠	Pass	5♣
	end			

♠ A 8 4
♡ J 10 3
◇ A K 10 6 3
♣ 7 2

♠ 9 6 3
♡ Q 9 7 6
◇ J 9 7 2
♣ K 6

Partner's opening bid promised 8–10 points with a six-card suit
headed by at least one of the three top honours and is likely to be
respectable within this range at this vulnerability. North's three
spades was directional-asking, requesting at least a half-stopper
in spades for no-trumps.

You lead the ♣6 to the ace, seven and jack. Declarer now
plays the ♣7 from dummy and when partner follows with the
three, finesses the queen to your king. How do you continue?

Let us roll-call the hand so far. Declarer is likely to have a minimum of seven clubs which will give him at least six tricks in that suit plus two top diamonds and the ♠A. The two top hearts are likely to be divided between the unseen hands, which implies that if South has the ♢Q he will get home easily unless she is a singleton. In that event, it will be difficult for South to avoid two heart losers and you can always lead a diamond at a later stage to cut declarer off from dummy. The critical case thus arises when South has two diamonds without the queen. (If he has three, he can make the contract with a restricted choice finesse against your jack after the singleton queen has dropped on the first round.) On that assumption, partner will have the ♡K (the ace would give him eleven points) leaving South with the ace in this layout:

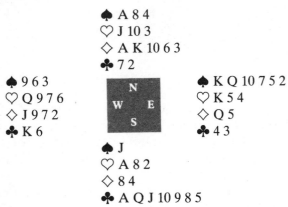

```
                    ♠ A 8 4
                    ♡ J 10 3
                    ♢ A K 10 6 3
                    ♣ 7 2
  ♠ 9 6 3                          ♠ K Q 10 7 5 2
  ♡ Q 9 7 6          N             ♡ K 5 4
  ♢ J 9 7 2      W       E         ♢ Q 5
  ♣ K 6              S             ♣ 4 3
                    ♠ J
                    ♡ A 8 2
                    ♢ 8 4
                    ♣ A Q J 10 9 8 5
```

Suppose you persist with spades. South ruffs and after drawing the second round of trumps, has little choice but to play for split heart honours, starting with a low one from hand. You will have to duck (or expose partner to a simple finesse) and partner will win. A diamond return is now too late (even ignoring that it gives a possible third trick in the suit immediately). Dummy wins, declarer returns to hand by ruffing dummy's last spade and runs the rest of the trumps. Left in sole charge of the red suits, you will be squeezed. To avoid this, you must attack diamonds at once and partner must continue the suit when in with the ♡K. Dummy is now isolated and declarer must concede three tricks.

It should be added that, as the cards lie, you will probably defeat the contract more easily if you allow the ♣Q to hold. Declarer is likely to cross to dummy in diamonds for a second trump finesse which you will win and now a second diamond finishes the hand without any need to be clever in hearts. However, this risks looking very silly if partner's doubleton club includes the jack. Nevertheless, there are similar situations where it does pay to duck in this position and this hand is yet another illustration of the importance of working out the whole hand at trick one. There is no time to think at trick two when you will have to play your low club at an even tempo to avoid giving the show away.

Hand No. 45

Dealer South
N–S vulnerable

W	N	E	S
			1♠
Pass	2♦	Pass	2♡
Pass	4♠	Pass	4NT
Pass	5♦	Dble	6♠
end			

♠ K 7 5
♡ K J 2
♦ Q 10 7 5
♣ A 7 4

♠ A Q J 10 6 2
♡ A Q 8 7
♦ 8
♣ Q 10

West leads the ♦6 to the five, jack and eight. East exits with the ♠8. How do you play?

You have ten top winners in the majors and the ♣A. Barring the unlikely contingency of a singleton ♣K, the twelfth trick can only come from a squeeze. You should realise that, although it is clear that East has the big diamonds, crediting him with the ♣K gives you no chance. As he is sitting over dummy, a simple squeeze is out and you are short of an entry for a ruffing squeeze. You must therefore realise that, if anyone is going to be squeezed, it will have to be West which implies giving him the ♣K and, despite the bidding, diamond control. There is one realistic chance only.

The full deal:

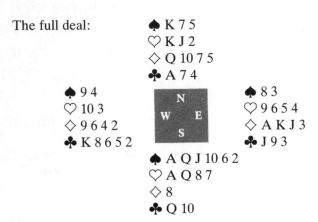

```
                  ♠ K 7 5
                  ♡ K J 2
                  ◇ Q 10 7 5
                  ♣ A 7 4
     ♠ 9 4                       ♠ 8 3
     ♡ 10 3          N           ♡ 9 6 5 4
     ◇ 9 6 4 2    W     E        ◇ A K J 3
     ♣ K 8 6 5 2     S           ♣ J 9 3
                  ♠ A Q J 10 6 2
                  ♡ A Q 8 7
                  ◇ 8
                  ♣ Q 10
```

If you play for the layout above, you will win the trump in dummy and play the ◇Q, forcing East to cover. Ruff, draw the other trumps and cross to the ♡K to lead the ◇10, again forcing East to cover. Ruff again and now, with West in sole charge of the diamonds, you can run your major winners. At trick eleven, you will lead your last trump (the two clubs are still in your hand and dummy has ♣A7 and ◇7). West will have to discard from ♣ K 8 and ◇9 and, whichever suit he discards, you will make the last two tricks.

Hand No. 46

Dealer East
Neither vulnerable

W	N	E	S
		Pass	1♡
Dble	2♡	2♠	3♣
Pass	3♢	Pass	4♡
end			

       ♠ Q 7
       ♡ Q 7 2
       ♢ K J 8 3
       ♣ 10 9 8 7

♠ A K 8 4
♡ K 8
♢ Q 9 7 2
♣ Q 6 5

South's three club bid was a long-suit trial asking for help in the suit. North's three diamonds expressed an indifferent view on the subject of clubs, but indicated his values in diamonds.

You cash your two top spades, partner following with the two and six and South with the five and ten. How do you continue?

Partner seems to have indicated a five-card suit and you should have noticed that his second card was the six, neither his highest nor his lowest, suggesting that he has nothing to help you in either minor, or a bit of both. As you have fourteen points, the opponents are in game and partner has already implied the ♠J, you know which it is—partner has picked up another of his famous rock-crushers! So you are on your own and can see the trump king as your third trick with every chance of the ♣Q providing the fourth. But now count South's tricks—four in hearts, two in clubs and three in diamonds, assuming he has a doubleton, making nine and as you will be in charge of both minors you will have to concede a tenth on the run of the trumps. You must therefore attack communications in a similar manner to the previous defensive hand, leading a low diamond now and another when in with the king of trumps.

The full deal:

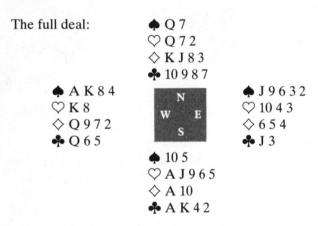

```
                        ♠ Q 7
                        ♡ Q 7 2
                        ◇ K J 8 3
                        ♣ 10 9 8 7
    ♠ A K 8 4                              ♠ J 9 6 3 2
    ♡ K 8                N                 ♡ 10 4 3
    ◇ Q 9 7 2        W        E            ◇ 6 5 4
    ♣ Q 6 5              S                 ♣ J 3
                        ♠ 10 5
                        ♡ A J 9 6 5
                        ◇ A 10
                        ♣ A K 4 2
```

Dummy is now cut off and nothing now can prevent you from scoring with the ♣Q.

Hand No. 47

Dealer West
Neither vulnerable

W	N	E	S
2♡	Pass	Pass	2♠
Pass	4♠	end	

♠ A 4 3
♡ 10 3 2
◇ K 9 6
♣ K J 9 8

♠ K Q 9 6 2
♡ A 8 7
◇ 10 3
♣ Q 10 3

West's opening bid showed 6–9 points and exactly six hearts to at least one of the top three honours.

West leads the ♣5. When you play low in dummy, East wins with the ace and returns the ♡Q. If you duck, there will be a ruff and immediate defeat, so you take your ace and cash the ♠K on which West drops the ten and East the three. How do you continue?

You can draw trumps now, finessing against East should West show out on the next round, giving you five tricks in that suit, three in clubs and the ♡A. Thus the ◇A will have to be with West, but even now you have entry problems. If you draw trumps and cash the clubs for a heart discard, there is no convenient entry back to hand and you will have to use your trump, allowing West to cash his hearts when in with the ◇A. Cashing clubs first risks defeat if a defender is able to ruff in early, even with the trumps 3–2.

The full deal:

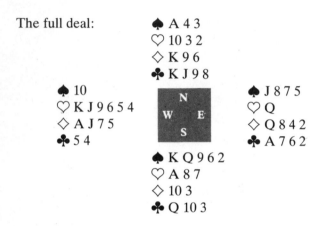

```
                    ♠ A 4 3
                    ♡ 10 3 2
                    ◇ K 9 6
                    ♣ K J 9 8
  ♠ 10                             ♠ J 8 7 5
  ♡ K J 9 6 5 4          N         ♡ Q
  ◇ A J 7 5          W       E     ◇ Q 8 4 2
  ♣ 5 4                  S         ♣ A 7 6 2
                    ♠ K Q 9 6 2
                    ♡ A 8 7
                    ◇ 10 3
                    ♣ Q 10 3
```

The solution lies in an endplay-squeeze against West. Draw trumps and cash the clubs, discarding a heart, even if it means finishing in dummy. On the last round, West will be down to ♡ K J 9 and ◇ A J. If he discards a diamond, you can safely play the suit from dummy, so he must discard a heart. You give him a heart trick, but ruff the next round and lead a diamond through his holding. On the above layout, cashing the clubs early works, but West could have had: ♠ 10 x ♡ K J 9 x x x ◇ A J x ♣ 5 x and now you go down when a simple line of drawing trumps, cashing the clubs, exiting in hearts and later leading a diamond towards the king would have been successful.

Hand No. 48

Dealer East
N–S vulnerable

W	N	E	S
		Pass	1♣
Pass	1♠	Pass	2NT
Pass	6NT	end	

♠ A Q J 10 7
♡ K 6 5
♢ A J 5
♣ J 3

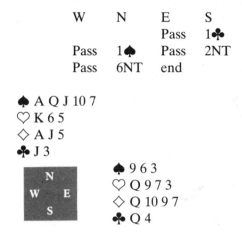

♠ 9 6 3
♡ Q 9 7 3
♢ Q 10 9 7
♣ Q 4

South showed 17–18 points.

Partner leads the ♣10 to the jack, queen and ace. South cashes the ♢K, all following low, and then a second round, finessing the jack to your queen, partner completing a peter. Have you any comment on the play so far and how do you continue?

The opponents have thirty-three or thirty-four points between them and you realise that once again, partner is loaded with goodies. Counting tricks, you can see two each in the minors, five top spades and at least two in hearts and thus there is little hope unless partner can provide the jack. Even now, you are in trouble. On the run of the spades, you will have to guard the diamonds, partner the clubs and therefore neither of you can keep three hearts—a straightforward double squeeze. Thus returning a club is out of the question and, as is usually the case when a double squeeze is threatened, you must attack the middle suit, hearts. A low card, however, will not be good enough if South holds ♡A 10 8. South may play low, setting up a finesse position against your queen. The only card to beat the contract is the ♡Q.

The full deal:

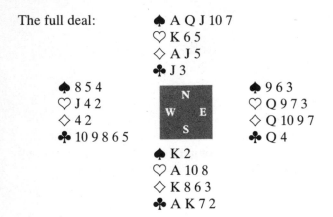

```
                  ♠ A Q J 10 7
                  ♡ K 6 5
                  ♢ A J 5
                  ♣ J 3
  ♠ 8 5 4                         ♠ 9 6 3
  ♡ J 4 2            N            ♡ Q 9 7 3
  ♢ 4 2          W     E          ♢ Q 10 9 7
  ♣ 10 9 8 6 5      S             ♣ Q 4
                  ♠ K 2
                  ♡ A 10 8
                  ♢ K 8 6 3
                  ♣ A K 7 2
```

South was too meticulous and the safety play against a singleton ♢Q in your hand was a false economy. If he takes the finesse at trick two, your ♡Q no longer hurts him. He wins in hand, cashes the ♣K and runs the spades. You have to keep diamonds and must therefore abandon hearts and now two top diamonds squeeze West in hearts and clubs.

Hand No. 49

Dealer East
N–S vulnerable

W	N	E	S
		Pass	2♣
Pass	2NT	Pass	3♠
Pass	4♦	Pass	4♡
Pass	5♦	Pass	6♣
Pass	6♡	Pass	7♠
end			

♠ 4 2
♡ K 6 3
♦ A K 5 2
♣ 9 7 6 2

♠ A K Q J 10 9
♡ A Q 8 7
♦ 3
♣ A Q

After a long series of cue-bids, you reach a grand slam and West leads the ◇10. How do you plan the play?

There are twelve tricks on top and it seems a simple matter of drawing trumps, testing the hearts, ending in dummy and now, if they break, you throw the ♣Q on the other top diamond and claim. If they don't, you take the club finesse and curse your bad luck if it fails.

The full deal:

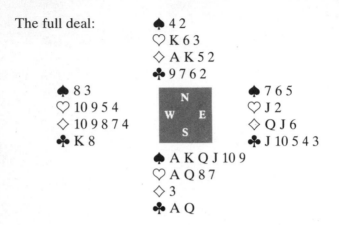

```
              ♠ 4 2
              ♡ K 6 3
              ◇ A K 5 2
              ♣ 9 7 6 2
♠ 8 3                          ♠ 7 6 5
♡ 10 9 5 4         N           ♡ J 2
◇ 10 9 8 7 4    W     E        ◇ Q J 6
♣ K 8              S           ♣ J 10 5 4 3
              ♠ A K Q J 10 9
              ♡ A Q 8 7
              ◇ 3
              ♣ A Q
```

But it isn't bad luck—it's bad play. If you are going to be a successful declarer, you have got to be the greediest pig in the sty; don't settle for a line of play giving sixty or seventy per cent when you can have eighty or ninety. Without jeopardising the simple options, you have squeeze chances against West in clubs and hearts, and diamonds could be involved as well. On winning the first trick, you should first ruff a diamond in hand. This isolates the diamond menace and now West is in charge of all three side-suits. Now you run the trumps and watch his discards. He can spare one diamond, but on the last two rounds he is finished. A red discard amounts to immediate surrender so he must discard both clubs—you do not even have to guess that he has blanked his king. This line of play must improve your chances by several per cent and with a grand slam at stake, must surely be worth the effort.

Hand No. 50

Dealer North
Both vulnerable

W	N	E	S
	Pass	1♣	Dble
Pass	1♡	Pass	2NT
Pass	3NT	end	

♠ K 6 4 3
♡ Q 9 4 3
◇ J 6
♣ 8 6 5

♠ 7 5 2
♡ 10 8 7 6
◇ 9 5 4 3
♣ 4 2

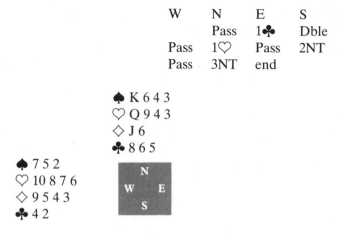

South is likely to have about 20–22 points more than you have!

You lead the ♣4 to the five, seven and three. Partner persists with the ♣9 and this time South takes his ace and attacks diamonds starting with the two to the five, jack and ace. Partner returns the ♣10, won by South's king; plan your defence.

You must choose your discard with care, particularly as you have learnt by now that hands like this often contain a surprising amount of defence. You should have noticed that partner, who obviously started with ♣ Q J 10 9 7, kept playing low cards, implying that his entries were in the red suits and thereby denying the ♠A. Giving him the ♡A implies that South cannot touch the suit without conceding five tricks and will need the spades to come in with the diamonds. That implies he will need the ♠Q and if he has a third card, he will be good for four spade tricks, two clubs and all will hang on the ◇10, irrespective of your defence. But clearly it would be unwise to discard a diamond now as partner might have started with ◇ A 10 doubleton. However, the diamonds may be solid for four tricks and now the critical case arises when South's spades are A Q doubleton. That leaves partner with ♠ J 10 9 8 and on the run of the diamonds, he will only be able to spare one of them and will be forced to release a club after which South can cash ♠ A Q and play on hearts, losing only four tricks. You must put partner in a position to release two or more spades by hanging on to your holding, the seven being high enough. The only safe discard is a heart.

The full deal:

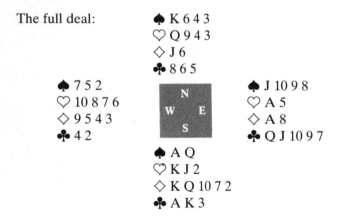

```
              ♠ K 6 4 3
              ♡ Q 9 4 3
              ◇ J 6
              ♣ 8 6 5
♠ 7 5 2                        ♠ J 10 9 8
♡ 10 8 7 6        N            ♡ A 5
◇ 9 5 4 3     W      E         ◇ A 8
♣ 4 2            S             ♣ Q J 10 9 7
              ♠ A Q
              ♡ K J 2
              ◇ K Q 10 7 2
              ♣ A K 3
```

Hand No. 51

Dealer East
Neither vulnerable

W	N	E	S
		Pass	1♣
2NT	3♡	Pass	4♣
Pass	5♣	end	

♠ A Q 9 6 4
♡ K 7
♢ 7 4 2
♣ A 5 3

♠ K 7
♡ A 8 5 3
♢ J 8
♣ K Q 9 8 7

West's overcall was the unusual no-trump, promising a red two-suiter. North's 3♡ was a cue-bid, looking for 3NT, promising a heart stop but denying a diamond stop.

West leads out three top diamonds, East following up the line. Plan the play.

West will probably be 5–5 in hearts and diamonds, leaving three cards in the black suits and you should realise that you cannot ruff hearts on dummy without being overruffed and therefore that the spades will have to come in to make this contract. That implies the likely need for a 3–3 break, leaving the clubs 5–0 as here:

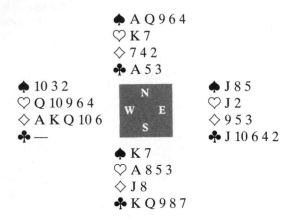

Thus you should ruff the third diamond, cash the ♡K and take a trump finesse. Now the ♡A and three top spades leave:

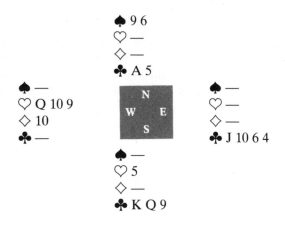

Now follows the ♠9 and whether East ruffs high or low, he cannot take a trick. This line also succeeds should West have started with a low club and doubleton spade.

Hand No. 52

Dealer South
N–S vulnerable

W	N	E	S
			1NT
Pass	2NT	Pass	3♡
Pass	6NT	end	

♠ A 5
♡ A Q 10
♢ K 8 6 3
♣ A Q J 10

♠ J 9 6
♡ K J 7 5
♢ A 4 2
♣ K 6 2

Your opening bid showed 12–14 points and partner's reply was Baron, asking for four-card suits, attempting to find a 4–4 or 4–5 minor suit fit. West leads the ♢Q and, irrespective of how you play to this trick, East discards the ♣5. Plan the play.

There are eleven tricks on top and except in the unlikely event of a defender holding ♠ K Q doubleton, the twelfth will have to come from a spade–diamond squeeze. It seems natural, therefore, to duck this trick to rectify the count on the assumption that West holds both spade honours. However, it will pay to consider other eventualities. You can see that, if East has both honours, there is no hope. But they may be split in which case you may be able to put pressure on West to blank his honour after which you can cash your ace and lead towards your jack. Thus you should play for a squeeze without the count, winning the first trick in hand. Then cash the clubs and three rounds of hearts, ending in hand, and provided neither suit breaks worse than 4–2, the following position will remain, H standing for honour:

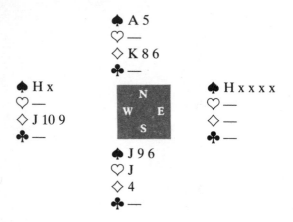

On the ♡J, if West discards a diamond, you discard the low spade from dummy, duck a diamond and claim. Thus he must discard a spade to allow you to discard a diamond and play spades as explained above.

The deal:

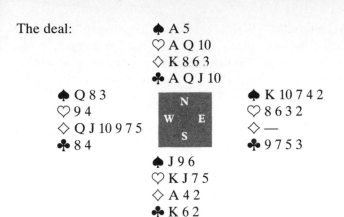

```
                    ♠ A 5
                    ♡ A Q 10
                    ◇ K 8 6 3
                    ♣ A Q J 10
    ♠ Q 8 3            N          ♠ K 10 7 4 2
    ♡ 9 4          W     E        ♡ 8 6 3 2
    ◇ Q J 10 9 7 5                ◇ —
    ♣ 8 4              S          ♣ 9 7 5 3
                    ♠ J 9 6
                    ♡ K J 7 5
                    ◇ A 4 2
                    ♣ K 6 2
```

Hand No. 53

Dealer East
Both vulnerable

W	N	E	S
		Pass	1NT
Pass	4NT	Pass	6NT
end			

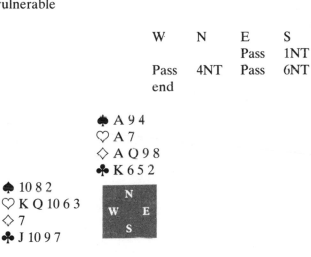

```
                    ♠ A 9 4
                    ♡ A 7
                    ◇ A Q 9 8
                    ♣ K 6 5 2
    ♠ 10 8 2           N
    ♡ K Q 10 6 3   W     E
    ◇ 7
    ♣ J 10 9 7        S
```

South's opening bid showed 15–17 and North's reply was quantitative. You lead the ♡K to the seven, five and two. How do you
continue?

Partner can hardly have more than a jack. If he has ◇ J 10 x x, the contract is doomed as South will not have enough tricks. If he has the ♡J, he will be able to look after the hearts and there will be no squeeze available to declarer. The critical situation lies in the probability of South having seven tricks in spades and diamonds, three in clubs and the ♡A to make eleven. In that case, you will be in sole charge of clubs and hearts and in danger of being squeezed. If South has three or more clubs in addition to the ♡J, there is nothing you can do, but there may be hope if the clubs are blocked as here:

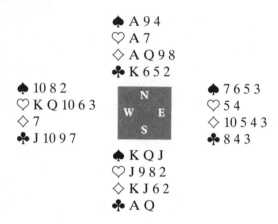

```
                  ♠ A 9 4
                  ♡ A 7
                  ◇ A Q 9 8
                  ♣ K 6 5 2
♠ 10 8 2                              ♠ 7 6 5 3
♡ K Q 10 6 3          N               ♡ 5 4
◇ 7              W         E          ◇ 10 5 4 3
♣ J 10 9 7            S               ♣ 8 4 3
                  ♠ K Q J
                  ♡ J 9 8 2
                  ◇ K J 6 2
                  ♣ A Q
```

Now a simple squeeze is ruled out and South's only hope is a criss-cross. To remove the necessary entry, you must attack the ace of hearts immediately by continuing the suit. Had you not led a heart originally, South could have got home by a criss-cross strip-squeeze, simply running his winners and setting up the suit you abandoned.

It is also worth noting that six diamonds cannot be beaten and it costs South nothing to start a Baron roll (i.e., bid his four-card suits upwards) in case there is a four–four fit.

Hand No. 54

Dealer East
N–S vulnerable

	W	N	E	S
			Pass	2NT
	Pass	6NT	end	

♠ K 8 3
♡ A K 9
♢ 10 8 7
♣ K 7 5 2

♠ A Q 7
♡ Q 7 5
♢ A K Q
♣ A J 9 3

West leads the ♡J. Plan the play.

'With nine solid tricks outside clubs, it is simply a question of ensuring three in that suit. The danger lies in West having Q 10 x x. I cannot be sure of the contract but there is a safety play if East's singleton turns out to be the eight.'

That was the way my thoughts ran as I played this hand in a recent team-of-four match. Consequently, I won the first trick in dummy and led a low club. The feeling of thrilled satisfaction when East produced the eight is hard to describe. I now had a perfect safety play to ensure the contract. Winning with the ace, I returned the three, inserting the seven when West played low to protect against this layout:

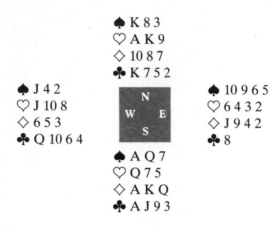

```
                    ♠ K 8 3
                    ♡ A K 9
                    ◇ 10 8 7
                    ♣ K 7 5 2
  ♠ J 4 2                          ♠ 10 9 6 5
  ♡ J 10 8          N              ♡ 6 4 3 2
  ◇ 6 5 3      W         E         ◇ J 9 4 2
  ♣ Q 10 6 4         S            ♣ 8
                    ♠ A Q 7
                    ♡ Q 7 5
                    ◇ A K Q
                    ♣ A J 9 3
```

That, of course, all happened in dreamland. Need I relate what befell me in real life? East actually held ♣ Q 10 8 and I claimed twelve tricks when the seven lost. As I wrote down the score, I was fairly confident that result would be repeated at the other table where a nationally-known name was sitting in my position. I was wrong! The bidding and lead were the same but the 'expert' concerned was not in the mood for clever safety plays. The ♡A was followed by the ♣K and a successful club finesse and an overtrick for a 1 i.m.p. gain . . . to win the match by a similar margin.

There are two places in this world you can guarantee never to get any justice . . . and the other is the law court!

Hand No. 55

Dealer East
Neither vulnerable

W	N	E	S
		Pass	5◇
end			

♠ 9 2
♡ A 7 4
◇ A
♣ K 10 7 5 4 3 2

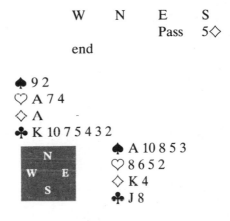

♠ A 10 8 5 3
♡ 8 6 5 2
◇ K 4
♣ J 8

Partner gets off to his usual devastating start by leading the ♣A, which South ruffs. Crossing to the ace of trumps, declarer adds insult to injury by discarding the ♠6 on the ♣K. He then ruffs a club and leads the ◇Q to your king, partner following. Can you save the day?

123

South is clearly short on points and must surely have the rest of the diamonds to justify his bid. So he started with eight trumps and a club void, leaving five major cards, one of which he has already discarded.

Turning to tricks, you can credit South with seven trumps, the ♣K and ♡A to give nine so far. Partner's insistence on leading an ace from A Q x x suggests that he has equally embarrassing holdings in the other suits and must therefore surely hold the ♠K without the queen. That implies that South will have no chance unless he has the king or queen–jack of hearts to put his total tricks to ten. In either case, the ten will have to be with partner; where South has K J 10, he is bound to get the two-way finesse right after that opening lead. With Q J 10, he doesn't even have a choice.

Thus South has to be 2–3–8–0 or 3–2–8–0. In the latter case, he has no chance so you must consider the layout below:

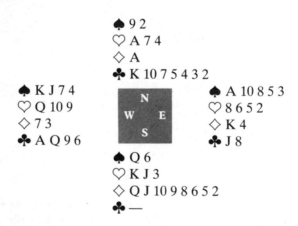

```
                    ♠ 9 2
                    ♡ A 7 4
                    ♢ A
                    ♣ K 10 7 5 4 3 2
♠ K J 7 4                              ♠ A 10 8 5 3
♡ Q 10 9            N                  ♡ 8 6 5 2
♢ 7 3          W        E              ♢ K 4
♣ A Q 9 6           S                  ♣ J 8
                    ♠ Q 6
                    ♡ K J 3
                    ♢ Q J 10 9 8 6 5 2
                    ♣ —
```

Observe the effect of trying to cash spade tricks. South will ruff the second round and run the trumps to squeeze partner in hearts and clubs.

Even cashing one top spade and then switching to a heart is not good enough. South will win in hand and the run of the trumps will still finish West. To ruin the entries for the squeeze, you must attack hearts immediately. South will try to counter, winning in hand and rectifying the count by playing a spade himself, but you will win and send back another heart forcing dummy's king, and now the club menace becomes harmless.

Following your brilliant effort, you can politely inform partner that, with all the side suits well stopped, a trump is probably the best lead in this type of situation. South will now certainly lose three tricks and if you attack hearts each time you are in, he will be held to nine.

Well, it has all been very hard work, but I hope the set of problems has illustrated the benefit of working out hands in detail and if it means that, just occasionally, you can go up and collect the prizes rather than applaud as others do so, I am sure that you will agree that the effort was worthwhile.